"…I believe Yong is guilty but I value Amde's opinion"

—07.03.2004

"I agree with your columnist Amde Sidik that the Special Task Force has been lukewarm in carrying off its task. Instead of deporting these illegal immigrants they are being given VIP treatment at detention centres…."

—03.04.2002

"…guest columnist Amde Sidik opined…the illegal now migrating to the interior." Chong Kah Kiat, former Chief Minister of Sabah,

—27.02.2002

"Don't forget the other top guns too, as your columnist—Amde Sidik said people want to see the outcome of the investigation of state public bodies, like SPA, Sawit, SAS management, etc…."

—07.04.2002

Sunday Forum-Daily Express

Writing

Writing

◆

from the tip of Borneo

Amde Sidik

iUniverse, Inc.

New York Lincoln Shanghai

Writing
from the tip of Borneo

iUniverse, Inc.

For information address:
iUniverse, Inc.
2021 Pine Lake Road, Suite 100
Lincoln, NE 68512
www.iuniverse.com

First Edition

Cover design and photo by Borneon House Production

ISBN: 0-595-32657-9

Printed in the United States of America

Contents

Preface

This book is a collection of articles over the last two years up to 2004. All articles here have appeared in my guest column of Daily Express-Malaysia except, chapter 27-letter to the Editor.

Never intended for compilation at the first place until a friend volunteered to do it. I realised later many articles that I wanted to include were nowhere to be found.

The idea to have these materials published perhaps is to serve as reminder and enables me to reflect back of how much things have changed over the years.

Written mostly under *a coconut tree*, so to speak, but I am not sure whether it would be any different if I wrote them on the top of Malaysia's Petronas Twin Tower.

The issues highlighted were of common knowledge in the state of Sabah, and Malaysia in general-typical dilemma in developing countries.

Among the example are, issues on illegal immigrants, national identity cards, corruption, cronyism and poverty.

I encountered a few problems at the early stage of my writings, some local authorities were not used to being criticised but I made myself available to them to debate what I wrote.

One or two did call.

The Sipitang *'tragedy'* was resulted from peoples' outcry regarding the federal road linking Beaufort to Sipitang. The road was less than 30 kilometres but the government could not even complete it, 36 years after British had left Sabah—the then called North Borneo. The very road leads to Kuching and Brunei-very important road for the community at this area indeed.

Another was when about 34,000 Malaysian Identity Cards (ICs) had not been collected in Sabah. The Registration Department had announced to destroy them had it not been highlighted in the media, I think many Sabahans would have no identity cards until today. The illegal immigrants got them as easy as buying *pisang goring* through unscrupulous local politicians.

Amdee Sidik
Sipitang   March 2002

Acknowledgements

My writings were done at leisure. But much of the inspirations came from many people including James Sarda, Charles Ayub, Kassim Supinah, Awang Saifuddin, Jainudin Jabidin, Kamis Daming, Kwik Harris Onik, Datuk Ayub Hj Aman, Zahir Ahmad, Mohidin Hj. Majin, Johnson Tee, Zulkhairi Hj Ismail, Hj. Hanif Ismail, Abdullah Yacob, Zareena Razi, Roger Balakan, Murshidie Hj Hamzah, Tahir Mohsein, Lawrence Muggang, Arimi Sidek, Mahmud Osman, Jaidin Tamin, Datuk Joe Leong, Munai Hj Mamit, Hj. Mat Arrifin Mat Isa, Mansur D Yassin, Rosnah Onek, William Chia, Cyril Pinso, Manaf Rahman, Bidin Latip, Clarence Sinsua, staff of Health and Welfare Division of Yayasan Sabah, Fauziah Sulaiman and Tracy Moinin who helped make compilation possible. (I know I missed some)

Last but not least those around me are: my wife Norida, my daughter Emieldza and my son Mohd Ameerul without their support I do not think I could be sitting under the *coconut tree* for too often.

Politics

1. ONLY THE FITTEST SURVIVE IN POLITICAL JUNGLE

10 February 2002

WHEN and in what situation do politicians have to use compromise as a means of settling their political wrangling—I mean, among members of the same political party or members of component party?

The answer: when the harmony of the members is likely to be disturbed or security of the country is at stake.

In other words, a political compromise is a must in order to avoid bad things from happening. What are the bad things? I am not sure, may be creating animosity and disunity among members.

Whilst another extreme example, has no connection to what I want to say later is, in time of war, politicians need to consolidate their energies together to safeguard the interest of the country. And politicians have to forget their personal interests.

In other words, political differences are in abeyance because of the love for the country.

Other than that, political compromise to me is unwarranted. Not only is challengeable by law but it is inappropriately and unfairly used.

Of course, it will only become an issue if and when the affected persons rise to challenge it.

Normally political compromise is created in order to avert the loggerheads among or between the leaders. It is a means, to avoid competition.

Yet we talk about everything else is democratic. We are living in a free country, but we are only free to do things so long as we do not challenge those who make the rules.

That is why some people say, in politics, only the fittest can survive in time of political upheaval. I agree, in the broader context. The fittest I mean the person who is not only durable but have sound understanding of the field. A *tahan lasak* politician? He or she is not only clever but continuingly in search to fulfil his or her political ambition. And the most importantly, he or she is a hard working one.

To me political compromise could only be accepted when neither side feels secure of winning. And because neither one of them wants to take the risk of losing.

Compromise means a method of reaching agreement in a dispute, by which each side surrenders something that it wants.

Even PM coerced to no election for the UMNO-United Malay National Organisation top post because he sees if a contest is allowed it could bring more harm than good.

Even though others see it differently which very often choose to be silent. I am sure they talk about it somewhere. And if any one dares to challenge PM, as we already know he will make sure he wins.

In the case of PBRS-Parti Bersatu Rakyat Sabah what Tan Sri Joseph Kurup should have done was to wipe out Datuk Dr Jeffery from the picture right from the beginning. He did not.

My contention is, if ever I feel I am at the upper hand why should I compromise at the first place?

Tan Sri Joseph Kurup introduced a kind of *half-democratic system* in PBRS. I see it half because the rest is allowed to participate in the election so long as the president's post is exempted. And there is nowhere he could convince others by saying that his motive of suspending Dr Jeffery was because of so...so...tactically it was a bit naive and showing sign of panicking.

On top of that, Datuk Dr Jeffery is a highly confidence person. As I mentioned above I would only compromise if I foresee risk as a result of my challenge.

To reach to a certain degree of confidence in oneself requires hard work. A daydream is not sufficient. I remember when I was a kid reading a Malay book, it was about a kid who used to have daydreaming while climbing a coconut tree. One day, he dreamt of rearing chicks, the chicks turned chickens and later he exchanged with goats later cows and becoming bigger and bigger. He sold them all. He became a rich man. Because he was so excited he took his hands off the tree. Of course, he fell down. That was *angan-angan* Mat Jenin and that is not enough.

I believe both the two leaders have worked very hard but at the material time Dr Jeffery seemed to be working doubly hard, that makes him enough members to support.

That working very hard business is so important and appropriately so plus intelligent, I know others also work very hard but less intelligent in case like this, things become shamble and at the end has no finishing. I quote it from one of my friends, Datuk…a former Minister.

Remember some time ago our CM—Chief Minister was referred as lame duck by our PM-Prime Minister. I interpreted that term as one does only when told, or does it for himself, or does nothing at all yet claimed to be doing for *rakya*t at the general election.

In the future Sabah needs not only hard working representatives with intelligent mind because t leaders are to lead.

I support the Yang Berhormat-YBs who work very hard for the people at the same time working very hard for himself. Because it shows good example and we called that leadership by example.

People also judge a leader based on his history of performance. If one has been holding a post for the last ten years seen only doing mediocre or next to nothing, than can we not say that his history is not good enough and we do not expect miracle from him given another ten years.

I believe once one is given the opportunities one should make a full use of it. In other words, capitalise it to the fullest.

While those who are no longer performing should say good bye—I agree to what DPM-Deputy Prime Minister statement recently. Keeping too long unproductive YB-Yang Berhormat (The Most Honourable) is just like keeping *batang buruk.*

2. CHONG EMERGES AS CLEANEST AMONG SABAH'S POLITICAL *POKEMONS?*

25 March 2001

IF all goes well, as it should we will be getting a new Chief Minister on Tuesday.

Datuk Chong Kah Kiat will be the 12th Chief Minister of Sabah and the sixth under the rotation system introduced by the BN government since in power (1994) about seven and half years ago.

Becoming the CM at 54 is not too bad. The survivor of Sabah politics, as some put it and the only leader from Berjaya Government of 1976-1985 when he served as the Assistant Minister to the Chief Minister.

About 5 weeks ago in this same column, it was mentioned that in the event that decision could not be made as to who would be selected from the Kadazandusun community, the choice could be from the Chinese Liberal Democratic Party-LDP or Sabah Progressive Party-SAPP.

I was not suggesting that there is no Kadazandusun leader capable to represent their community or perhaps because the Kadazandusun was seen disorganized at the present political scenario.

Thus the PM wants to cool it down. But if it is the case, I do not see the reason why the formula has to be changed.

The major components BN parties was given a two-year term each but the new formula is two terms for UMNO and one each for Chinese and Kadazandusun.

For what ever it is, since all parties involved have agreed that PM is to have the final say then I find the squabbles are rather unnecessary for any political parties.

The PM is given the final say and has said it. Unless Sabah politicians do not mean what they say, and such practice is not only tricky but also it really is a bad habit.

I would always subscribe to the idea that if one does not agree one has state his case.

I do not see there is a need to emphasize that whatever we do has to be based on race and religion. Many ordinary people whom I know for sure do not like the idea of selecting leadership based on racial background.

Are we not seen just as bad as reverting to dark ages? Of course the PM would say, that his decision was based on after taken everything into account.

Coming back to the issue of our new Chief Minister, I think there are a few things that the ordinary people expect Datuk Chong CM—ship to be concentrating on in the early stages. Among other things are:

- Lessen the problems, uncertainties—a kind of mess in the administration of the state. A lot of indecisiveness in past resulted in bottlenecks for Sabah economic development.

- We are still lacking of transparency in as far as running the government departments and government agencies for examples: Saham Sabah-SAS, Sabah Port Authority-SPA, Sabah Palm Oil-SAWIT, etc

Of course the power of CM is not unlimited. He could only go to certain extend. But on the strength of the record that Datuk Chong as Minister of Tourism (I mentioned in this column 3.12.2000) I would say he is so far among the cleanest YB, and this could set a fine example to the people in term of confidence as some of those who became CMs turned out to be no more than pocket monsters (pokemon) when the various deals they signed became public knowledge not to mention controversies.

I do not expect Chong to change his colours or style throughout his two-year term. In any case, as they say, successive Sabah CMs have been having a field day signing away the timber, seafront, hills and lands that today there is nothing much left except contracts.

I also see Chong doing a good job if there is no interference.

Civil servants alike want to see a clear direction in as far as the state economic policy and social priorities are concerned.

Selection on those who would hold important position in running the government agencies should based on merit. Otherwise it would affect the credibility of the government. Reduce the uncles, aunts and best friends factor. Appoint somewhere need appointment and filled the vacancies that needs filling.

When people are happy the country will have fewer problems.

To cite an example, I went to a remote kampong in the Sabah one day and I pitied a kampong folk walking using rubber sandals in the thick jungle. Thus I suggested to him that I would buy him a pair of rubber shoes to replace the sandals.

To my astonishment he did not want the shoes. He said he was happy with sandal but he would prefer *parang* instead.

Thus the best decision come from knowledge of the subject. Until and unless we find out we are only guessing.

One can therefore be rest assured and forget about the oppositionists and the opportunists for a while, as after all they can never agree.

3. History will judge rotation of Chief Minister (CM) of Sabah

4 March 2001

WHETHER the rotation of the CM is on or scrapped only the Prime Minister knows. I notice people from different backgrounds tend to reason differently about the issue. A member from a different political party would answer along his or her political believes.

The PM said one of the weaknesses of the system is that it tends to create a series of "lame duck" chief ministers. This is after the system has been implemented for nearly seven years.

Lame duck means a person who can do nothing without the help of others or simply ineffective. That is quite a harsh word judgment for a number one leader of our state. It could also mean that Sabahans are not good enough?

Datuk Yong Teck Lee one of the former CMs responded by saying that for the past seven years the system is deemed to have been a suitable formula to cater for Sabah's unique political situation.

Lame duck issue could only arise in the final few months of the CM's two-year term. But I have to add every final few months in the office of CM—in any office of power—is akin to a rush—rush situation. Whether it is of two-year term or five-year term makes no difference.

In a way, people are concerned about CM's power. Sabah has experienced having very powerful CMs in the past. Thus the powerful CMs will make things worse towards the end of his term?

People are worried if one day we ever get a "greedy" CM who would do everything within has power to get things done for his advantage before leaving office. In the end, State's resources are gone with him. In that scenario we have only ourselves to blame.

Our *kayu balak* is a classic example. A venue for misappropriation of State's property in the past, contracts have been awarded to cronies and relatives. Ordinarily poor people have no land, land alone own *kayu balak* while, a great number of our ministers and former ministers own hundreds if not thousands of hectares.

Datuk Harris *(former CM)* mentioned recently about alienation of open space in front of the Kinabalu police station where there is a "funny looking building". I was told nobody touched this area before, not until the introduction of rotation CMs.

Many, even government officers joke that one-day Kota Kinabalu's roundabout and road partitions would have building on them.

As for the building referred to by Harris, I cannot blame him because where on earth does one find a police station wholly cut off from public view.

Tan Sri Bernard Dompok said it is the Cabinet that needs to be strong. Power dos not purely rest on the CM. I think it would be fairer to go by the book but it does not always happen.

Some people think the rotation serves as a mechanism to avoid the abuse of position whoever the CM is. Is such concern justified? To some yes, when our State's resources are depleting every moment, if no careful planning is made we have nothing left for the next generation. We even heard about a mining possibility in Maliau Basin.

University Malaysia Sabah-UMS could at least come up with a survey to indicate whether people at large prefer rotation or otherwise. It could enlighten the public by having an academic approach to look at the problem, very commonly we talk of being proactive but we are bad in practice.

A top senior civil servant scolded his officers by saying he or she cannot perform but only good at talking.

My view is, these days there are plenty of junior officers with better concepts of good management except they have no means to exploit and practice the ideas.

Some promotions or rewards are not based on merit but because he or she has an uncle and untie, or close friend.

Most UMNO members, the dominant partner in BN, feel the rotation system should be done away with. But the tricky bit is they want their own UMNO 'horse' as CM for whatever reason.

For me this is just as good or as bad as having rotation. So better have rotation. What about the ordinary people—the voters in the state? What do they think about the system?

The Rotation was an arbitrary decision and was at least expected at that time. Of course, again there is no obvious right or wrong decision as of now. History would judge us perhaps 50 years later.

4. CHIEF MINISTERS COME AND GO BUT ISSUES LINGER

11 February 2001

IN less than two months we may have a new Chief Minister by virtue of promise made by the Prime Minister of Malaysia to rotate the Chief ministership. An unusual political arrangement tailored for Sabah.

Of course, the announcement of the new Chief Minister is eagerly awaited. And the guessing game will go on for a while.

Will the same person continue? If so than the Prime Minister is breaking his promise. If he breaks the mother of promise that might not augur well for Sabah.

The State's politics and economic stability hinges on his words and action; the time to be cautious is no more right than at this time when the Government is facing tough challenge from the opposition.

Next, if the promise is kept, who will than be the new Chief Minister? It could be PBRS (judging from their greater number of assemblymen) or from LDP or SAPP (in the event he decided to allow the Chinese to have their turn to allow the Kadazandusun to sort it out between BPRS and UPKO-United arty Kadazan Organisation and maybe even calling a snap poll should the KDM-Kadazan Dusun Murut side be undecided by the end of Chinese term)

Meanwhile let's talk about issues that are going to remain uniquely unsolved should the current CM leaves the office.

The two that cannot be taken out of peoples' mind for sometime are the Saham Sabah, the Sabah Ports Authority's loans and the mater meters.

For this column I only deal with SAS as it directly affect 60,000 voters, not including their families, relatives and friends.

The SAS issue has been lingering for sometime now it could damage the credibility of the BN's State government.

The state government has failed to convince majority of the people that it has no business with SAS. And SAS management has all the time appeared numb and unresponsive to queries.

Yet again, politicians never fail to talk all the time about people's participation and transparent government. All this so far is in contrast with the concept of caring government, preaching and practicing runs opposite direction.

So also with the concept of freedom of expression, one is free to say in theory, but what is the point in saying when no one would bother to listen.

The frustration is manifested in the media, especially in Forum. Though what I see represents only very small group of people, nevertheless sufficient to warrant attention.

In the case of Saham Sabah (SAS), the state government has neither direct say nor direct responsibility in as far as its daily running, in theory at least. But the SAS management is.

It is equally true that business of this nature involves risk. At the end of the day one either makes money or losses money. That line of argument could be accepted by many people, but the issue at hand is that people want to hear what and if SAS has anything at all to say in relation to:

- How prudent and diligent the management of SAS is in looking after the investors' interest;

- How if 'doctrine' of transparency is at work.

One-way of enlightening the people are by telling them of the real position and that the management has done everything in good faith.

There is a genuine concern that the authority must respond to the outcry. Otherwise, people would not appreciate any future dealing of this nature. Do not blame them. But blame the blamable.

The prudent management team is the keeper of public trust because it involved public interest.

Five years ago, this management team campaigned from kampong to kampong, inviting people to invest, with a promise of good return. Some kampong folks who had account elsewhere, like in the ASN or AS diverted their account to SAS.

Firstly, because of the promise, second, out of love for Sabah and proud to be associated with Sabah's achievements.

Because of strong persuasion, assurance and strong recommendation of backing by the BN State Government, they never imagine that the RM 1,000 they invested five years ago would only be worth RM 190 if they withdraw today-a loss of RM810!

One year has passed since the present Chief Minister assured the public not be unduly worried because the State Government will back it by pumping in money to ensure the price does not slide further.

Last year was .23 cents per share and today is .19 cents per share. There is no sign of recovery nor assistance to put SAS back on track or at least an effort to minimize further slide.

Many assumed that the announcement made by the Chief Minister last year was rumored to keep the price at RM 1.00 per unit that would bring some relief to many investors but that hope too, short-lived.

As analyst commented that to put the price around 0.50 cents per share now which means, a recovery of .18 cents at the Kuala Lumpur Stock Exchange-KLSE would require SAS around RM 125 million to be injected into the fund. Whose job is this?

About 59,000 investors invested their money into SAS. Some had put their hard earned money like, life saving and pension money.

From the first day of campaign during the tenure of Datuk Salleh Said Keruak, people were under the impression that the state government was behind. No effort was made by SAS to clarify.

Soon afterwards, the management of SAS has departed from the conventional way of managing fund of this kind, that is, when 61.4 of RM 360 million were put in only two counters—the NBT for 8.4% and REPCO for 8.6% and nearly 40% of its investment were in the second board for everyone knows second board is always volatile.

In the conventional method, SAS should not have invested more than 5% of the total value into one single counter. Had SAS taken prudent approach by investing only 5% into a single counter at that time, the situation would not have been as disastrous as it is today.

Since 1997 the price per share has been hovering around .25 cents when other funds could easily paid dividend around 6%.

Will there be any rescue? In the case of Malaysia Airline System-MAS, the authority topped half of the value, which was seen incredibly generous. But what has happened to MAS may or may not necessarily happen to SAS. The only similarity is they were the creation and placed under the purview of the BN Government.

My other question is, since most of our Muslim leaders have been preaching the so-called moral virtues, adhere to religious teaching, even the 'recreation activities' that akin to gambling activity is considered immoral, I for one will support it.

But the moment the State's own agency gets involved in investing people's money in a company like REPCO which had link to gambling, it makes me wonder.

Though in this case, the choice is up to the individual but I am referring to the preaching.

In conclusion, the people have the right to know the true picture of how SAS managed the their money.

5. IF SABAH POLITICIANS DON'T UNDERGO CHANGE—
Creative rather than intelligent minds

3 December 2000

THE talk among *kedai kopi analysis* these days is mostly about the Sabah economy and where it is heading.

Economists, bankers, politicians and lawyers argue but their presence actually creates more confusion than solving the problem.

In the end, they do not really talk about economic as *per se* but merely over viewing the roots of economic difficulties.

I do not even understand the question fully, let alone to give satisfactory answer. Yet I cannot escape without saying anything either as they would nag me.

I shall not attempt to answer like the way economist does; instead, I just want to highlight some points, if these have any bearing to our economy disarray.

In the past, we relied so heavily on timber. At one time Sabah was the richest state of Malaysia because of timber. I remember well as student from Sabah whenever we got chance to visit the peninsular we bound to hear remark '*oh…he or she is the son or daughter of balak tycoon*'.

We were the mistaken identity. Of course, Sabah timber produced several millionaires.

In those days to get rich, one just have to build good connection with those in power, be nice to politicians if not be one and locate the concession and you are soon on the road to being a millionaire.

Which reminds me of a remark made by one[1] of the district officers a few months ago.

He said it was unfair for rural districts like Nabawan to be deprived of development, (he meant, infrastructure) when these districts had provided wealth to the country for decades-from *kayu balak*.

I will add to that. In my observation, many of our rural roads, roads that were built by timber companies/contractors for the purpose of transporting timbers out of the jungle are now neither repaired nor maintained.

Many bridges are gone missing because the timber contractors are no longer there.

These roads are vital to the rural people like in Salarom, Pengaraan, Layon-Pensiangan, Nabawan, Torontongan and Nawonon in Ranau[2]. No roads mean no link to outside world.

No timber companies in operation also mean no jobs for rural people nearby.

Most likely they would stay at home doing exactly like what they did before the country's independence.

---

1. Nabawan's District Officer, reported in the Daily Express, 2000
2. Rural people living in the interior like Salarom, Pengaraan, Layon-Pensiangan and Nabawan, Torontongan and Nawonon in Ranau.

Worse, they cannot go into the jungle to hunt for wild animal for food anymore without being hassled.

I for one do not blame the wild life officials but I feel disappointed when they could not catch the encroachers in the broad daylight who enter the protected jungle to shoot *tambadau*[3] and *payau* alike. I myself have not seen one *tambadau* yet, so what chance would our newly born have?

I know one senior officer[4] who loves to keep the horns of these animals for home decoration.

Can we not imagine that rural people in the interior could not even take bath in the river let alone drink?

In Long Pasia, some five years ago, the water of Matang River was nearly crystal clear but now it is just as milky as tea *tarik*.

On top of that, many thousand hectares of our land are still barren[5]; surely the promise for re plantation has not been fulfilled.

Only last week another far cry from rural people of Nabawan appeared in the *Daily Express* under the heading "Refugees in our own State"

The report said outsiders were given many hectares of land whilst their request was denied.

Soon our jungles are all gone to make way for oil palm plantations. Will oil palm products secure sales?

Tawau smallholders are now experiencing the pinch when mill owners refuse to take the oil palm seeds; mind you it only takes 48 hours for the seeds to rot.

Our jungle soon is replaced by *acacia mangium* plantation in the case of Benta Wawasan to make way for pulp and paper mills.

I am very sceptical about re plantation, we have seen this with our own eyes besides, and it takes about twenty years to be 'fully matured[6]'.

What would happen in between time and even if the trees are all matured it cannot be same again the issue is because of the sheer size.

It is said to provide 6,000 jobs but in our experience again, it is very unlikely that the 6,000 jobs to be filled up by local unless something is created to attract them.

In the end, more illegal foreigners are coming would be attracted here and just in time for another State general election.

---

3.   Wild buffalo?
4.   One Senior Officer from Peninsular Malaysia instructed his officer to get the horn of *payau* to be sent to KL
5.   One can see this on the way to Long Pasia
6.   To be a *full pledge jungle like*?

Life is getting tougher. Our economy is not moving far from where we were since the recent economic meltdown.

The younger generation started to blame our previous leaders because they did not prepare much groundwork economically for the next generation.

Timber is sure depleted, no apparent replacement to it.

Mineral, like copper in Ranau is already history and to seek gold or coal in Maliau Basin or Danum Valley is surely a fiery issue.

In layman's terms, the question asked is to mean what kind of business activities that can generate income for the state.

What about oil? Yes, this one is interesting topic; our oil has made reasonable contribution to the wealth of our nation.

This is why the 5% in return as royalty for indefinite period are an issue.

I think there should be a review.

The twenty points, which are frequently mentioned, are in fact good guidelines for our leaders to fall back on.

If changes must take place then it must be for the benefit and harmony of both parties-the state and federal. Otherwise any move is seen as sinister.

I am convinced from the available documents[7] so far that most major decision for the state had not been thought out in much detail unlike what Lee Kuan Yew did for Singapore.

Our previous leaders were not good enough at negotation[8] nor they were competitive when facing more experienced politicians from Peninsula.

This is further exemplified as in the recent handing over of Petrajaya to Federal Territory, Selangor will receive RM200 millions compensation plus RM7 million yearly for indefinite period.

How much did Sabah get for Labuan?

Come back to the issue of economy, Sabah has big land area, plentiful of marine life and fisheries. Of course, this is no straightforward transaction.

We need creative minds, rather than intelligent ones to convert into cash. If a country like Switzerland can survive on tourism industry, I see no reason why Sabah cannot-except that we do not think like Swiss.

Sabah has unlimited range of attractions for foreign tourists.

Agriculture, aqua culture—fisheries and tourism are the ones that ready to be fully explored. I see the Ministry of Tourism has done a good job despite of kidnapping problem. Congratulation!

7.　Among them is the biography of Lee Kuan Yew
8.　I have not found any document indicating that they had serious debate on the issue.

Capitalizing on our land use is the right direction. I know much has been said about it.

Mohd Fauzi Patel last week in his column proposed to try on buffaloes rearing. I agree. This time *buffaloes boleh.*

We need investors. Likewise, local companies must be sufficiently big in order to create an impact in the state.

We are lacking in both. We are left with institutions like, branches of banks, insurance and couple of small factories whose presence does not contribute multiplier affect.

In other words, money is not shared around. What collected by branches is sent back to their headquarters. Thus, the amount of money they have is just enough to keep them going no more no less.

How good is KKIP—Kota Kinabalu Industrial Project in providing such facilities one may ask?

The land price is a bit too high to entice both local and foreign investors according to some business people.

Our electricity and water supply are chaotic.

Sabah has also lost millions for having foreigners like Filipinos and Indonesians in the state.

Imagine Rm50.00 a month sent by one in every ten of the foreigners in the state to their respective country.

And there are 600,000 as told in Parliament.

By the look of it, if there is no change in the perception of our leaders Sabah is going to remain like this for many more years to come.

6. Identify as Malaysian instead of race

3 August 1999

SABAH has about 29 different ethnic groups, the biggest of all the states in Malaysia (Sarawak 20 and Peninsular Malaysia 5[9])

As Sabahan, I am proud to say that we are able to live harmoniously for many years without any racial or communal infighting. Many foreign countries envy us. Many foreigners find that this is special, and many want to emulate our style.

Malaysian has managed to show to the world that we are peace-loving people, despite of diversities.

---

9.   Sarawak: Magnificent and Mystical, pp.xiii, Vinpress Sdn.Bhd, Kuala Lumpur, 1994

I have been asked by many people when I was in overseas, what are the magic formula that enables Malaysia to stay quiet all along—no industrial strikes, no green peace interference, etc. Are Malaysians that cool?

Looking deeply at our success, I would say it was and is very much to do with the human factors.

Cultures, religions and determination of the people for better life have contributed to the maintenance of peace and harmony of our country.

Whilst the political system of governance has no doubt played a significant role. It augured well for the past 36 years since Malaysia independent. And 42 years Federated Malay States independent; no major racial upheaval happened, like those experienced by Kosovo, Khasmir or some in former Soviet Union and in many African nations, except the May 13, 1969 in Kuala Lumpur.

The May 13, incident taught us a great lesson of how dangerous ethnic and religious intolerance could be.

In the context of Sabah, we have no experienced in racial confrontation, not even the May 13. The news of the incident did not even reach Sabah until it was over.

In the context of Sabah, we have not experienced racial confrontation, not even a May 13. The news of the incident did not even reached Sabah until it was over. There could well be fighting in the seas prior to independent time. But this was caused by the sea-faring people-piracy, mainly from nearby islands of Philippines and Indonesia.

The Brunei people too were good at sea but they were more interested in trades than anything else.

For example, during the reign of Majapahit[10], and no history of them being involved in pirating.

Brunei Sultanate[11] had a strong army in the 1700s. When the British East India Company fell into the hand of Sultan Sulu (in Balambangan), its Chief Staff (John Herbert), had to stay in Labuan.

The Suluk did not dare to attack Labuan because earlier Datu Teting the Sultan Sulu men were defeated by Pengiran Temanggung of the Brunei Army.

In the mainland of Sabah, there had been a few rebellions. The famous ones were rebellions led by Mat Salleh, Sharrif Osman, Si Gunting and Robert Kwok. All fought against the colonialists—the foreigners.

---

10. Awang Ahmad, *Dewan Bahasa Brunei*, Januari 1978
11. Amde Sidik, "Labuan " unpublished materials, 1998

The 1962 revolt[12] in Brunei and surrounding the Brunei Bay of Sabah and Sarawak, as many writers put it, that revolt was against Brunei Sultan, and at the same time against the formation of Malaysia.

Intermarriages among them were very common which is still true today.

One great tradition of the people of Borneo was honesty. Many years ago, it was a common sight along many roads in Sabah, especially in the interior, the local people selling their products without even manning them.

One would find the vegetable sellers hang empty cans or coconut shells or cut bamboo stem besides their products to put your money for payment—still happens in some parts of Sabah.

Therefore the concept of trust living in a multi-racial society is and was not new to us. We have practiced the tradition as long as we can remember.

But many of our noble traditions are dying out due to power, money, rules and regulations.

We know democracy gives people not only right to vote, but also political and civil right to fulfil the needs.

The issue is, even the most authoritarian regime claim they are acting on behalf of the majority, and say, it is democratic.

Our constitution spells out the citizens' rights and freedom.

But as always, the politicians interpret and apply it in according to the order of the day.

Of course, there is no perfect system and every system has limitations. It took Britain[13] 150 years to have a fully developed parliamentarian system what it has today. One can imagine what stage is ours.

When our new generation seeks clarification because there is a different between what they understand and what is being practiced, our reply therefore has to be fair. We cannot simply assume these people are against the establishments or government.

Come back to multi racial issue, in Sabah, political system is mirroring the Peninsular set up, like father like son situation. PBS, UPKO, PBRS Kadazan/Dusun/Murut, UMNO the Malay the rest of Muslim community and SAPP, LDP the Chinese.

Our cabinet Ministers are still frequently be identified as Malay or Bajau Minister, Chinese Minister, Kadazan Minister and so on.

---

12. W.C Walker, *Background to a Revolt: Brunei and the Surrounding Territory,* Sarawak Museum, 1963
13. Asiaweek, August 20-27 1999

The common argument they would say is, because the Malay Minister knows the Malay people best, so also the rest.

I would consider that once he or she is appointed as minister, the ministership is for the entire state or country.

No individual community has more rights over another.

We also notice that coming from the same race does not necessarily be the best *wakil.*

7. SABAH NEVER FACED PROBLEM CONCERNING UNITY—STATE GENERAL ELECTION 1999

14 March 1999

I HAVE been attending, some political *ceramahs* both the government and the opposition political parties. My summing up is, among the hottest topics in any *ceramah* so far are:

- Advice on unity by politicians,

- Kuala Lumpur not colonizing Sabah

- The importance of development,

  and

- Interests of Sabahan must be Safeguarded.

Politicians are saying in so many ways how dangerous disunity is especially in time like this. In other words, we cannot afford to be disintegrated.

We are facing—Soros…economic downturn; we must therefore consolidate our energy and rebuild our economy as quick as possible.

But the issue I am looking closely is, are we really disunited or disintegrated? Because the real people in the ground do not look as said by many politicians.

Some of the people who give ceramah are unfamiliar with the local people.

Both the people from Peninsula and Borneo still have plenty to learn. So far, too much talk about it but little were and are done to understand each other.

Failing to do that, any future political campaigns will always going to be the same and ever going tough.

Is there any different, the unity found among the people in Peninsula and the unity one found in Sabah or Borneo?

Sabahan do not find that they are or were disunited, as claimed by many politicians.

I would say, it is the politicians who have problem of understanding unity, or perhaps they do it on purpose to get attraction or they say it to create sensation.

To put it straight, there has been no major problem about unity. Historical records shows be it during the pre and the post independent of Malaysia, there had been no major upheaval found in Sabah based on racial or communal misunderstandings.

I mentioned earlier, in previous article that Mat Salleh revolted against the whites was because of colonial as well as divide and rule issues.

There is a basis for misunderstanding the issue of unity, in Sabah. This is acceptable, Sabah is more than thousand miles away from Peninsula, culturally there is a vast different between the two parts of Malaysia. Sabah has 29 ethnic groupings as well as many religious beliefs.

Though with such cultural and religious diversities, Sabah experienced no ethnic warfare unlike, the 13 May of 1968 found in Peninsula. There had been no incident that Sabahan were disunited or at war with one another.

Why?

In Sabah, it is common to find that, in a family they are made up of different races as well as different religions, yet they are living under the 'same roof'.

I am therefore of the opinion that, if the politicians are so disgruntle about the issue of unity, why can they make full use of Jabatan Perpaduan Negera?

In our context, even without this institution we are already united.

In my view, this particular institution has not done much work to improve the 'disunity' as claimed by politicians.

It methods of integrating people have not been effective, in the eyes of many Sabahan and Sarawakian; it is much more of assimilation rather than integration.

To make integration works it must involve two ways' responses. Each of them must be allowed to participate freely, venues and facilities must be provided to make them understand each other, physical environment like visiting or exchanging work place could take one example one unique culture of Borneo people that can easily misinterpret unless one understands it, in Lawas the 5th Division of Sarawak, it used to be a common sight to find an older generation of the non Muslim wearing *songkok*.

Anyone who is not familiar with that culture can easily be mistaken, that these people are Muslim, because it is perceived by many only the Muslims wear songkok. Wrong.

So when I heard the *ceramah* about unity, I consider these politicians have very little knowledge about the subject, they are there only to sentimentalise the environment.

They are narrow minded, ignorant and talking a complete nonsense!

Saying disunited just because one has different political ideology, hardly fits the description.

As Malay saying says, *tak kenal maka tak cinta* that means if you do not know the person you can not simply love him or her, fair enough.

But I think if one does not know much about the subject might as well.

8. SUDDENLY NO SIGN OF *GAWAT*—STATE GENERAL ELECTION 1999

11 March 1999

SOMETIMES we find it a bit too much, the way politicking is taking place in the election time like this. But that is how politicians going about capturing the hearts and the mind of the voters.

It does not make sense, and it baffles logic. Look at the television programmes these days. Many parts of Sabah were unheard of before, and all of a sudden becomes the darling of media. Is this not too artificial?

It has been a very long time since we last saw the Kadazan and the Murut dances and songs in the television. But now we hear and see it almost every hour.

The intense television coverage of Sabah was and is only done during the election time. After that we have to wait for another five years.

I asked friends how they felt and most said they did not take it seriously. Sometimes it is noticeable the commentators do not even know what they are talking about. Like mentioning a new mosque is in Tuaran when the fact is that it's Likas and a lot of twisting facts and figures.

Suddenly, there is a lot of money to go around. No sign of economic *gawat*?

But wait until after the election. To get that actual money released will require a lot more work or even arm-twisting. How many of these promises can be realistically be fulfilled?

Would it not be easy, more realistic and less suspicious if politicians have done their jobs before the end of the term, not to leave it to the last minute. So this campaign time is merely a touching up?

Most policy statements were not made in a normal way but through promises made during the election campaign. Some are initiated during this campaign time in as far as the Government's side is concerned.

For the oppositions everything is a still blank, so we are living on hopes.

Every candidate is saying he or she is only interested in *rakyat*. Anything that is good for *rakyat*, country and nation.

Perpaduan is important issue and always an evergreen issue sometimes known as bersatu (unity). The Government side does not like to use the word because the terminology is more connected to PBS.

So much advice about *berpadu* has been given as if we have not *berpadu* all this while. Sometimes it can be annoying or boring to listen especially in the house-to-house campaign.

I think a lot more listeners know what the term means than the person talking about it. The way they say it can create disharmony instead of harmony. Situation is worse when the talk is given by some one whom they have never seen prior to this campaign or not coming from the same locality.

Perpaduan in Sabah has been in existence long even before institution like, *Jabatan Perpaduan Negera* has been established. The people of this country were already *berpadu*. They had no problem. It requires no more telling.

Sabah is and was very special indeed when compare with other states in Malaysia. There was no incident for any racial upheaval in as far as history can tell. Mat Salleh revolted against the whites on the issue of colonialism and the divide and rule situation.

During the communist insurgency, Sabah did not have a single communist guerrilla.

No Kadazan fought against the Bajau and no Bajau fought against the Kadayan or Brunei for that matter.

The message is, politician should be prepared when giving talk otherwise one will find a lot of yawning going on at the back row.

Kampong people do not like arguments either, more so, if one is using somebody's house. Such a character if it happens can be construed as Sabah Medical Centre, Kota Kinabalu.

I was hospitalised for three weeks thus managed to watch TV programme.

9. Leaders are to lead

24 March 2002

AT a recent *kedai kopi* rendezvous, our group of five talked about the issue of performance of our political leadership in the State.

A few days earlier with a different group, we talked about the same topic, but the discussion was a bit restrictive, taking time between teeing off. The members could not argue much.

One, it was a bit in hurry. Second, because they were worried about forgetting the right swing for the next tee off and lost their bets. Especially when accompanied by one YB[14] who used to bring many thousands ringgits of cash in his pocket, sometimes brought an assistant to carry his black briefcase and betted almost every hole.

Now come back to the former, everyone presence agreed to pick one name quickly, just to make sure that the discussion was done before the glasses of *tea tarik* dried.

The obvious was, none other than Datuk Chong Kah Kiat who is half way into his full term in office as the Chief Minister of Sabah.

As always my friends were quite eager to reveal their assessment. But I got to ask them politely to hold their breaths. While trying to remember the pledges made by Datuk Chong at the beginning of the term. What are those pledges?

I will just mention some that caught the interest of these people. Among others are: issue on the illegal immigrants, issue on transparency—the lopsided agreement in the government agencies and promise to disclose the findings of the investigation. I reminded my friends that actually I do not know Datuk Chong personally unlike the previous four of CMs.

But by the same token, I just do what I have to do—write from the bottom of my heart. Tell the truth. Nothing but the truth. No, I do not have any other motives; there is no good ground for others to accuse me of *angkat kaki*.

The so-called assessment I refer to earlier is basically the deduction from information gathered from the chitchats, the gossips, whispers (said Fauzi Patel) and comments from ordinary people on the street, *kedai kopi* and golf course alike.

If it sounds trivial I am sorry but this is the cheapest method of gathering information as well as getting feedback from masses. Sometimes it is genuine and reliable depending on the source.

---

14.   I know the YB personally and for sure. He is not from Sabah.

Just to reflect a little bit, Datuk Chung is the 6th CM under the BN rotation system introduced the Prime Minister in 1994. And Datuk Chong was the least expected to be appointed as Sabah CM at that time.

Now he has passed half way, and this is where I feel the two-year term in the office, as CM is a factor. Too short the period. It almost ends before it even begins. Equally worrying is the 'thinking gap' from one Chief Minister to another. If it is too far a part it surely jeopardises all the good work done earlier.

A friend of Datuk Chung mentioned to me the other day, he remembers Datuk Chung once said; "Today I came to the office, opened my briefcase and did my work. By the end my term I'll come to the office for the last day, and close my briefcase off I go."

I am not very sure what that meant, but I interpret it this way—he does not stay forever as CM. So while holding the CM ship he feels he should do it properly and in no uncertain terms.

To me that is straightforward. He has a mission to accomplish.

As far as the assessment mentioned earlier Datuk Chong record is so far so good. Majority of our people understand being a CM. He has no licence to do everything he likes.

Datuk Chong has done something visible on the issue of illegal immigrants, pledge number one.

Suffice to say, in politics as in law, he has the intention to do something—he promised to do. He is now seen doing it. The next one is the result.

Of course now we hear loud and clear other political leaders pledging their support. It is also well known to us many are only good at *sokong* but very few become prime movers.

I raise the issue because the function of a leader among others is to lead. Not just *sokong*. Some of course, *cuba-cuba* (try) to lead but it is sad to say that *cuba-cuba* takes so long—until the end of three to four terms of office.

We have leaders who have dependent syndrome mentality, no clear directions and lack of conviction. This is what has happened to the issue of illegal immigrants.

It has never really been done in the manner it should. So many bottlenecks in the past hindered the implementation of the task.

Datuk Lajim rightly commented recently that no one should be given a preferential treatment in connection with one Merotai Assemblyman's call that fives colonies be spared.

I too received a SMS message[15], two days ago from Tuaran telling me that a group of people begged the police not to disturb a hundred or so illegal immigrants in that area-imagine the difficulty.

Datuk Chong has the support from people. I consider this is something of an achievement and surely to be long remembered. Plus with the help Federal Authorities the act now is no more right than any other time and it should be no turning back.

Equally true if the nation is to recover from the so much sorrowful events in the last five years, started with the economic crash in 1997, Anwar Ibrahim saga and September 11, in the USA.

Our political leaders must now come up with creative thinking, creative approach to rebuild the confidence of the people, the industry and the socio-economic. Most importantly, it all starts with political will.

Give the able people chances to build the nation and root out those unproductive leaders who only add to the numbers. Sabah needs competitive mind in both the Dewan and Parliament. I find it disgusting to hear when Sabah YB[16] started behaving loudmouths in Parliament but little substance.

On the issue of transparency in Sabah, the government must be seen practicing it for good governance. It is not just the company directors or accountants who could read or interpret the financial statement these days.

People who are entrusted to manage our public sectors are mostly our highly paid civil servants. They therefore, are answerable to any loss of money due to unintelligent dealings like transfer of shares, which resulted unaccountable loss, unsolicited and one-sided agreement alike.

People would want to see the outcome of the investigation of the Sabah Port Authority, the transfer to shares to the one-ringgit company in SAWIT, Water mater issue, SAS management, etc. These discrepancies in the management of public agencies cannot be swept under the carpet. The public may be patient enough if matter is in the pipeline waiting for action.

But the bullying cannot go on for long. In real democratic rule, what the electorate give, the electorate can take away.

---

15. A family friend, a police, from Tuaran, informed me.
16. Bung Moktar Radin (Have you heard?)

10. AFTER SADDAM…

20 April 2003

HOW much longer before we know the fate of Saddam Hussein. But we do know from the media that the USA army and its allies are already in total control of Iraq. Are Iraqis' long days going to be over?

Soon the USA and its allies would claim the *proprietary right* as the 'liberator'. This is a new political doctrine made by *mad* politicians.

But first and foremost, the task now is to install the first governor[17] of Iraq. Bush has already decided—a former army general by the name of Jay Garner. The Governor? Yes, the governor who would later decide who get what and how much, especially on the oil contracts.

Only the USA and it allies will get. Countries opposed to the invasion would have no say. That is the rule.

The story of Western control over Arab countries in Middle East is nothing new. Time and time again history repeats itself and Iraq is no exception.

For the British, involvement in this war is a revisit[18]. They took control over Iraq in 1914-1918. It was the British, which renamed Iraq from formerly known Mesopotamia. They appointed the first King of modern Iraq, an Arab prince by the name of King Faisal I.

It is not surprising why Blair becomes staunched supporter of Bush. He does not want to miss the boat. Many if not most of Arab nations were historically under British protectorate at one time or another, for example, Iraq itself, Kuwait, Qatar, Bahrain Jordan, while others at least had had British officers as advisers.

The British mapped the Arab world; they did so in order to accommodate country like Israel in 1930s by disorienting Jordan, Syria and others.

Now Iraq is almost demolished, paralysed and flattened. The costs of this destruction are colossal, immeasurable and incalculable.

In the first place it was unnecessary losses to properties and infrastructure of the country.

Imagine, about 4000 BC the city of Baghdad was once the center of world civilization, up to the raise of Arab Empire in 752AD under Abu Jafur Al Mansur. The city played a central role for Islamic civilization.

---

17.   Fortune, April 7/No.5
18.   World Book 199

It was also the world's first known civilization and early cultures developed along Tigris and Euphrates rivers. By the year 800 Baghdad had already one million people, the center of trades and cultures.

The Ottoman Empire ended by the helped of British. The British at the time considered that was the right time to demolish the strong influence of Islam in the globe.

The fact is, without the British and Western allies many Arab Kings and Kingdoms were not be enjoying the power that now they have.

From this prospective it is difficult to see Arab nations could be fully committed in forming solidarity among them. Their political leaders have too much individual self-interests and power hunger, and today they are just as fickle minded, as they were many hundreds years ago.

The result of war ruined Iraq cities horrendously, with rampant and indiscriminately bombing by the allied forces, many hundreds, if not thousands innocent civilians were killed. While, those survived will be scarred in mind and hearts until they die.

Not everything that can be compensated in monetary term even if Bush has 80 billions ready.

Pictures and images of war in Iraq are updated after every few seconds globally in the media; televisions, Internet screens and newspapers, just like bullets and bombs showering the city of Baghdad.

Need no further explanations; journalists are hunger for news while the viewers and readers want to see and read the latest development of the war.

Viewers and readers do have choice as to what channel to see and what newspapers to read but on the whole, the contents of the media are almost alike, after all, they are basically from the same source.

All television channel stations and newspaper owned by the few well-connected people with interests. For this reason some journalists may not be able to write as free as they wanted to.

Journalists who do not conform to the media owners' aspiration are risking their career. A few tried to tell the truth and no sooner than later their respective countries branded them as unpatriotic.

This shows media is a medium for political propaganda. An example, PeterArnett[19] the Pulitzer Prize Winner from CNN and a few more were sacked for telling too much—a heavy price to pay indeed.

---

19. CNN Reporter

The CNN, BBC, CNBC are most popularly viewed in the region but unfortunately people from the third world's look at them as a real mouthpiece of USA and British government and seen serving their political masters.

In other words, they are machines for propaganda campaign to win the war. For people who have no background knowledge of the events would likely to sink by their rhetoric.

Of lately, the Arab channel Al-Jazeera, an odd one became more popular not only in Arab world but also for international viewers. Because it is showing something that others are not.

It has angered Bush administration when it showed the USA army-the prisoners of war are being shown as the footage.

Bush administration alleged that the channel has in breached of the Geneva Convention.

Ironically, it was only fourteen days ago the USA and its allies have broken international norms and rules, by invading Iraq—a cry from international community fallen into deaf ears.

One editorial[20] of regional magazine questioned, "What international law has been broken by the USA and its allies? No law says that the USA cannot invade Iraq"

I consider this is a dangerous statement. Surely if norm and treaties no longer law, what safeguard would to the world communities have? I am sure soon there would be more invasions like this to come.

Equally there is no mention in UN Charter that any leaders who are in breach to UN resolution have to be killed or his country has to be invaded.

If the provision is silent it does not mean they can do what they like. But again unfortunately it was the USA and Britain, which spearheaded the breach.

The USA may argue that there is no specific international law that has been breached, while for many people instruments such as convention and treaties are just as important as specific law.

It is chillingly frightening if this view of super power is adopted. I think Al Qaeda membership will not only be multiplied but also diversified.

The USA has given a wrong reason for invading Iraq by saying because of Al Qaeda connection when they could not even prove it.

For the majority of the Iraqis even if the battle is over, the uncertainty of stable Iraq is going to be for sometime—gloomy and dim scenario or may be bullets and bombs would still decide their fate.

---

20.   Far Eastern Economic Review, April 03,2003

Meanwhile, we in Malaysia many thousands miles away from Baghdad, we did not hear the bombs drop; we did not hear the moan, the groan and scream.

We only read and saw pictures and images of Iraqis sufferings, yet it was enough to make us sick. Some could not even sleep properly at night.

I cannot help but wonder how Bush, Blair, Howard and their allies could.

11. SABAH'S OPPOSITION ARE A BUNCH OF NO-HOPERS

25 January 2004

COMPARE to many previous state election. Sabah's opposition parties are at their weakest this time round.

Thus, whether the election is held now or in five month's time would not make much difference.

None of Sabah political opposition parties so far have created an impact that likely to shift people's opinion drastically from now up to election time.

Should the general election is held tomorrow there is not much controversial or explosive debates to attract voters. This would be a great disadvantage when they should be portraying their colours by now.

They should have laid some foundations. For example, explaining voters about their views in various fields. They should be able to challenge the existing government policies, provide critical analysis on the current policies as well as those policies, which have been implemented, participate in public debates, provide their view on how to manage the State economically, socially or politically.

The opposition's views on corruption surely need to be heard which was highlighted by Prime Minister recently, police inquiry, stoppage of one mega railway project, that is on the national level but what about our local level? So on and so forth, which people eagerly, want to hear. Such critical analysis would help people to see how sound, how serious and how prepared these people are.

So far the opposition have not provided good grounds as to why people must vote for them. I would imagine only miracle could change the fate overnight, but again miracle though it happened in the past does not happen too often.

Their intelligent discussions would helped provide a yardstick, whether one would stay voting the same party or switch to the new one.

Likewise sound debate with substance would make political campaign lively; otherwise the campaign fare this time would become a mere gossip *kampong*.

Due to absence of choice, casting a vote this time is only a formality. That would lead many to think casting a vote would make no difference since the winner is predicted.

The only real reason why people have to cast their votes is worried of being branded as unfriendly to the ruling political parties or even *considered* anti government.

The most common scenario in the state is that opposition parties appear only a few days before election time or some rather reappear just a few days before nomination of candidates, only to disappear again as soon as the election is over.

Such behaviour is only benefited the ruling parties.

Being opposition is not as rosy as one would expect, especially in this part of the world. The sacrifice is too big and too risky.

People in opposition have been stripped naked economically as in Singapore. That is why Sabah politicians switched parties the moment they feel the heat.

As nation grows and becomes more sophisticated, we should be seeing political maturity heading this direction, meaning, opposition political parties exist not just to wrestle power overnight, but rather planned and natured over a period of time.

Gone is the old thinking of forming a government overnight, once then reap every opportunity and abuse position.

Some budding politicians still have that mentality for self-enrichment first under the pretext that they are struggling for *rakyat*.

Another typical trait of our leaders once in power is the tendency of making people think only the leaders are right and not giving the people a chance to think for themselves.

Worst of all, failing to adhere to the idea, ordinary people who have no political affiliation are indirectly *bribed* by our leaders, for example, assistant which ordinary person is entitled to have could be withdrawn because he or she is seen unfriendly, anti government and unpatriotic.

The lack of intelligent opposition, it is not only make democracy artificial but also makes a nation half dead, losses its lustre, for the good of the country, and its people.

So in as far as Sabah is concerned, we left with opposition parties Keadilan, DAP-Democratic Action Party and PAS-Parti Islam Se Malaysia.

Everyone knows this opposition political parties are from peninsular. Of the three DAP has had a history and produced an MP in Sabah.

As for the latter many would think they would not be able to win a seat, let alone to form a government. But both DAP and PAS are durable oppositions unlike those found in Sabah.

Thus I do not think they dream of forming a state government yet but in other states the thinking is on.

Again, confining my discussion on Sabah based opposition political parties, and if I were the person who has the final say in declaring the date of election, my concern would be more to do with logistic and smooth administration of the election rather than about worrying losing the election to opposition.

This trend started during United Sabah National Organisation—USNO time and repeated during BERJAYA, PBS and BN now.

The opposition never last very long, why is it so? The people who created these political parties have never thought much beyond election time.

Unlike Peninsular opposition parties—PAS and DAP.

The idea of having opposition party is not solely to form a government within a very short space of time but rather to be a body which able to check and help monitor the administration of a country.

Otherwise, those holding power would go overboard as well as bigheaded. We have seen many examples across the globe, let alone in Sabah's own political history.

Playing a role as watchdog should be considered as noble. It opens up people's mind and provides space for improvement.

It also provides alternative view for people at large.

The other weakest side of being in opposition is of course lack of resources. Unlike in western countries being millionaires does not mean having to be nice to the ruling party.

This is because people are rather independent of government tokens or projects.

The next important element is the lack of credibility and integrity of the opposition leaders. Many wanting to be leaders were and are not up to the mark, some from old guards whose mind were tested and credibility is equally depleted as his or her age.

I am not saying those leaders in the ruling parties are super credible leaders. Some are mediocre, by flux and became YBs but hung on because of the 'big brothers' would pick him or her as candidates.

Contribution from opposition parties is almost zero. We oppose their very existence.

Socio-Economic and Cultures

12. MIGRATION TO INTERIOR

24 February 2002

HOW to get rid of those thousands of foreign children schooling in our government and government aided schools in Sabah?

The Education Director General Datuk Hj Abd Rafie He Mahat recently commented that schoolchildren of foreigners would be allowed to continue their studies in the government schools until the status of the parents is determined.

I wonder how long will this take. In our experience action taken by authorities is not normally instantaneous.

Our former Chief Minister, Datuk Harris Salleh said about 30,000 of them. They were the children of 60,000 Filipinos from the earlier refugees who crossed into Sabah in early 1970s. I wonder if this was the number of true refugees.

But the staggering figure on amount of State's expenses spent on the detention centres to feed the illegal immigrants RM 2.5 and another RM600, 000 on transportation is unjustifiably unfair to our rural people.

They are in great need of money to uplift their standard of living. Imagine these rural people do not even have enough basic food like rice[1] to supplement their daily diet.

And if people still pity the plight of the immigrants than imagine the cost to provide facilities and maintenance of the facilities for that lot, until the completion of (fifth form) *tingkatan lima* that is, for the period of 11 years.

The headline 'visible decline in illegal' last Sunday in the Daily Express struck my mind.

Their random survey shows a mark reduction of Filipinos immigrants in the city.

---

1. The writer has visited some villages like, Kg. Taringai Laut in Kudat and Kg. Saliku and Kg Seliliran in Pensiangan-Sabah. Unlike many of us they eat tapioca instead of rice-the choice of no choice.

My suspicion is, while it may be true the number of illegal declines in the Kota Kinabalu. But check must be made to see if the number does not swell up in Keningau or in Sipitang.

My guess, they might be migrating to the rural areas of the State.

I am glad to know that the National Registration Department now has gone to the interior of Sabah I have in fact highlighted this matter several times in this column.

I am quite sure that still a large number of our local people with no identity cards like the 62 years old Butor Anduhut[2] from Seliliran, Pensiangan.

I think many more will come out to apply if they are informed about the importance of having identity cards.

The next, we are equally concern with another group of immigrants. They are the Indonesians, largely from Sulawesi, Flores and Timor islands.

There have been unofficial reports saying that even in our higher Educational Institutions[3] have large numbers of non-local by origin but they could easily fall under the local category and they filled up the local quota system.

Because they are Muslims and because they look like local?

Unlike the Filipinos, the Indonesians in the other hand have en routed to our schools in a steady and successful manner for many years.

Perhaps by now they could be hundreds if not thousands already graduated from local Universities without you and me realising it.

The Indonesians are good in mixing and assimilating themselves with the locals.

Very often they can easily build connection with local leaders, especially with local politicians.

I remember one in Sipitang an Indonesian-Bugis was appointed, as Ketua Kampong.

Of course there was an outcry from kampong people. That, I think is short-sightedness on the part of our leader.

Come back to the foreign children issue, the difficulty in getting rid of these children is because the matter has not just started overnight, the rampant abuse of positions by our local leaders.

They issued passes and they produced fake identity cards, fake birth certificates, etc. Few politicians were detained under Internal Security Act but by the

---

2.   See New Strait Times, page 1, 18 February 2002
3.   UITM and University Malaysia Sabah

time they are out of the detention they seem to be enjoying facilities provided by the government.

Some were even awarded millions ringgit worth of government contract. So where does the decent man go from here?

This matter has been overlooked for a very long time to some people it almost tantamount to condoning.

During our State or Parliament election our local leaders were desperate for votes. They were therefore using these immigrants or illegal immigrants. This was not just something come out of the blue. It has been planned[4] and timed. Many documents, which have become public domain, are to be found easily to prove of such activities[5] exist.

Now do they expect to be sent home, after fulfilling the *obligation*?

Right to vote is the highest right that a citizen can have. An immigrant giving a reason like that can easily confront our immigration officer or Police officer.

Or sometimes officers have no recourse except playing a bullying tactic.

For example incident like, Mr ABC owned a Malaysian international passport, of course through a devious means, then one day he lost it. Mr ABC reported to the relevant authorities and wanted to get a replacement.

The Immigration officer is suspicious as to the identity, through no fault of his but previous the officer.

The common the reply given to Mr ABC is by saying the reference of your passport is lost cannot be found or that passport was a fake one?

Mr ABC is at loss. He insists he has a valid passport thus he roams around in Kota Kinabalu.

Datuk Harris is in favour of letting these children continue their schooling in the State. Otherwise he said these children would have no future if they were taken away.

Obviously this is a humanistic approach of solving the problem.

One can see the difficulty face by these children. But at the same time can we effort not to do anything much longer?

The status of refugee under the auspices of UNHCR cannot run perpetually. Our political leaders must settle with the international body.

UPKO lauded this issue sometime last year, which should be followed up.

It is also unfair and unjust for the people of Sabah to be made like second-class citizens.

---

4.   Abdul Mutalib Mohd Daud, IC Palsu, Januari 1999
5.   Judgment by Muhamad Kamil Awang, Kota Kinabalu High Court (8.6.2001)

For example their right to own an identity card have been ignored, when we now are about to throw it away, to be replaced by *mykad?*

Do not expect them to know *Mykad* at this stage, when our JPJ and police officers are not even sure how *Mykad* works, who is equally ignorant (DPM recent remark New Strait Times-NST, 18.2.2002)

We the NGOs have raised our concern for a long time on the immigrants' issue but I notice if it were not of Nilai's[6] incident in Peninsular perhaps immigrants' issue would remain as it was.

In as far as Sabahans are concerned the statement made by the DPM, Datuk Abdullah Badawi recently, that children of migrant workers are not allowed to enroll at government or government schools, is nothing if not clearer now-a big full stop.

13. *OF* HONORARY PhDS AND HARD-EARNED PhDS

3 February 2002

AN academic qualification is one of the oldest yardsticks for identifying intellectual capability of a person in his or her chosen field.

In England, this method dates far back as 1100s when University of Oxford was created, followed by the University of Cambridge in 1200s.

These Universities were given the right to give "license", which in the 1300s became what we now know as degree[7].

A degree qualification is know-how in theoretical aspects or interest rather than practical value of a subject.

A minimum period of three years for full time is required to complete an undergraduate degree-with reference to UK system, and must passed all the examinations prescribed by the University or College for graduation.

Knowledge is imparted through lectures and tutorials as well as some elementary research work in the case of first degree.

Common entry requirement to a first-degree course one must have a formal academic qualification, before 1993 it was O and A level and for Malaysian the Sijil Pelajaran Malaysia and Sijil Tinggi Pelajaran Malaysia.

---

6.   Indonesian immigrants (textiles workers) rampaged in Nilai in Negari Sembilan
7.   Derived from model of Guild system (UK) in 1300s

In the last few centuries another new term came up which is called professional qualification though nearly similar to academic qualification but of a very specialized nature for doctors, lawyers, accountants, quantity surveyor, architect, etc.

Professional qualification normally takes longer time to complete compare to academic qualification; for example, to earn an MD a person has to study a few more years compare with non-professional qualification. A law graduate has to take up another examination after completion of a first degree and has to do the chambering.

Or to become a fully qualified accountant one has to serve for a number of years in an accounting firm before he or she is entitled to use the title ACCA at the end of his or her name.

It is with academic qualification or professional qualification nowadays that separate Mr. A and Mr. B in the job market.

Concerned parents these days want their children to be only in the best schools, no matter what it cost.

In real world, for all intents and purposes, both fields are no longer one hundred percent true in as far as job matching is concerned. In a country where every field is governed indirectly by cronyism, nepotism and corruption, merit and quality of a person is no longer that important. Some would say it is whom you know that matters.

Also equally true, that mismatch of qualification against the task that one is doing is no longer a big deal. Or could it be, pick anything where there is opportunity.

It is no longer strange to find a microbiologist becomes a general manager of a bank, a law graduate ended becoming a very successful fabric designer or a medical doctor become building contractor, and the most successful politicians having no academic degree in politics, etc.

Nevertheless, whether the qualification they obtained were academic or professional, they have the privilege of adding titles such as BA, LLB, MD, MA, MBA and Ph.D. after their names if they so wish. Sometimes they are required to put down these credentials in formal manner in official occasions.

The title can only be used after graduation has taken place-a dignified and colorful ceremonial, unless of course, one receives the scroll in absentia by request as usually many of us who wanted to rush home after completed the course.

Lately, I observed a rampant inappropriateness of using such titles. There is no problem with undergraduate and postmaster qualification but it is the Ph.D., in short, styled *Dr* that bothers some people as well as creates confusion to public at large.

What really a Ph.D. (Doctor of Philosophy) or Doctorate is?

It is a hard-earned qualification because it has to be obtained formally.

A student has to be enrolled in *the institution* (University or College) doing course work as well as research. Or sometimes it is done purely on research work.

A university confers Ph.D. to a successful student; usually by spending several years in advance study of a specialized field by writing an acceptable dissertation and passing numerous vigorous examinations. A student must show through their work a significant original contribution to the knowledge.

An Honorary Degree is obtained quite in different manner. It is voluntary in nature. The most common honorary title given to non-academician is Doctorate of Letters (Litter arum), which styled as Hon DLitt[8] and Ph.D. is also not uncommon.

A person who is conferred with Honorary Ph.D. Degree need not have academic qualification, no academic work required, no transcript is issued and no academic subject is mentioned on the certificate.

Though mentioned may be is the graduate's contribution to a particular field of his or her endeavors, for example, "in recognition of services to the local community" in some cases honorary Ph.D. was rewarded as retirement gift or award for special occasion.

It does not signify any academic work but a special privilege.

For example, in one foreign university[9] in its manual for honorary awards and titles has this among its recognition:

- Taking particular account of the connection between the recipient and the University,

- The recipient earnest desire to promote public good.

- A person who holds Master or Doctoral shall only be considered for honorary at doctoral level.

- A person considered for an honorary award at master or doctoral level if the person does not hold a tertiary qualification or holds a qualification up to the level of bachelor.

---

8. This format is also shown in the list of Honorary Degree recipients of Macquarie University
9. The Charles Stuart University, manual for Honorary Awards and Titles

- A person who is nationally eminent shall normally be considered for honorary award at doctorate level.

- A person who is being recognized for service at a regional or community levels the "unsung heroes" shall only be awarded at Master level. The list goes on...

Honorary degree for Undergraduate, Masters and the Ph.D. degree has along standing history nearly every university in the world has awarded Honorary Degree to people like celebrities, politicians, members of business community and philanthropies alike.

Our eminent persons are no less popular in the eyes of the world today; many therefore have been awarded with honorary Ph.D. in their fields of interests by both foreign and local universities, for their services to the community and the country.

I am here merely concerned about the way the title being portrayed.

The recipient must know when and how to use the title, which otherwise people who know about it would find it uneasy. For example if one is awarded a honorary Ph.D. in the field of say, Ecology surely he or she must have a little bit of knowledge in Ecology but obviously not as scientific or systematic as the hard earned Ph.D. unless he or she has already got a Ph.D. academically in the same field.

Therefore, in the eyes of academician the honorary Ph.D. cannot be equated as a non-honorary Ph.D. unless as mentioned above.

I have seen on papers that some eminent figures can have as many as five or more honorary Ph.D. or Doctorate awards beside academic Ph.D. That must be eminent! He is qualified to be addressed as Dr because has the academic one already.

But for one without academic Doctorate and to be addressed or called like one would create a bad impression on him or her and the institution, which readily presented this.

It is not unusual to find that a person with only an honorary Ph.D. is not call a Doctor as such. Or usually a person is reluctant to put the title Dr in front of his name.

To distinguish between the academically earned Ph.D. and the honorary Ph.D. or Doctorate in document form, in most instances[10] is, by inserting the

---

10.   Refer to Calendar 2001/2002, Emeritus Professors and Distinguished.... University of Exeter, UK

word (Hon) in front of the title, after the name for example, XYZ, BA, MA, Ph.D., Hon Ph.D. or Dr XYZ or Mr. XYZ Hon Ph.D.....

Conventionally and ethically this has been the practice in the world.

14. Hard to be objective-NGOs' leaders

29 April 2001

FOR a serious person running an association can never be an easy job.

To accomplish it requires energy, stamina and resources. The association that I am referring to is an ethnic association or any community based associations.

I remember well some years ago a few of my Kedayan friends approached me and requested me to help revived Sabah Kedayan Association. At that time, the association was already de registered.

I did not take much interest then because an ethnic association to me sounds a bit too *racial*, but somehow these friends of mine managed to persuade me.

The argument on race bothers me at the beginning but later I began to see differently. I consider an ethnic association is just like a big family, for example, where some of the kids are left far behind whilst some move too far ahead.

Thus the issue is how can the better-exposed group in the family assist the under privileged ones and play a role for the good of the family.

I notice many other ethnic associations changed their names or even inserted a word like *Kebudayan* or *Kebajikan* (culture or welfare) in addition to the name because of fear of being called racist.

I consider that unnecessary because it is well within the law of the country neither do I feel a shame just because it shows my race.

At the same scenario, the larger racial group including the Malay keeps on saying the importance of its race. So, I would consider a smaller group like mine is no less entitled to claim its importance.

At the end of the day, only the Kedayan knows the Kedayans best, so also applies to other ethnic groups in Sabah.

Since then I learnt a few things, I know more about my root. And the more I understand about them the easier it becomes for me when and if I have something to deal with them.

My earlier anticipation was just to assist my friends to get the association registered, and hope that at the later stage someone else could start the ball rolling.

But things changed, the persons who help registered the association has to be responsible in running it as well.

And later I realized that not many would like to commit wholeheartedly and objectively to run an association from stretch which no sure way of success. In fact, an association like mine could also make life more miserable since there is no apparent benefit at foresight.

To date still many associations have never had bank account in the bank to be legally allowed to receive, keep and transact money for their activities. Which means managing an association like this is far from proper, when money is the main ingredient for an association's success.

Unlike running students' association which many of us did during our school, college or university time, the ethnic association has bigger scope and much more complicated, vast different in the make up of membership and greater variation of expectations.

Whilst running students' association activities not only it is smaller in membership but also all we know the whole objective is just for students per see.

I still recall the student's activities that I have involved with as a member of Malaysia Students' Society in the UK and Eire.

Sometimes I envied those in the associations because they were so good at procedures when there were conferences and meeting alike. That is obviously beneficial for real working life.

Of all that I had been with, the Sabah Students' Union in the UK and Ireland was among the memorable ones. The Sabah Students' Union was at its peak in 1970-80s, the most active in organizing welfare and social activities for fellow students in the UK and Ireland.

It had in fact produced many of our state's leadership. Among those by—products of the Students' Union the former Chief Minister Datuk Yong Teck Lee (the last batch), Datuk Anifah Aman, Jalil Ghani, Datuk Zaki Gusmiah.

During my Presidency of the Union, Yong Teck Lee (now DatukYB) was the Union's Secretary General, others active participants just to quote some of the names are: Datuk Than Nyip Shim, Datuk Raymond Tan, Johnson Tee, Dr Frederick Chong, Dr Tan Kok Sui, Haji Mohd Hanif Ismail, Datuk Masidi Manjun, Jimmy Wong Su Peng, Datuk Ambrose Lee, Haji Abu Bakar Yahaya, He Bungga Burut, Joseph Wong, Kassim Supinah, Mohd Aid Datuk Ahmad and Mohd Hanan Ramli.

We were clear cut what we wanted to accomplish as students' leaders at the time—basically to carry out social activities to break the monotonous and mundane lectures at the campus.

The students' society served as focal point of meeting with other students, it also served as leadership training ground.

Whilst in case of the ethnic association a lot of misconceptions, some people at the kampong level assumed that the association is just another form of political institution, and its activities are intermingles with political activities of course, some can be true, some in the past even used his or her association as springboard to catapults him or her in a political limelight.

To some it is not, that is why it is difficult for any leader to be very objective.

15. DON'T DISMISS IMMIGRANT TAKEOVER OF LOCAL ECONOMY

11 March 2001

THE issue of foreigners[11] is hard to ignore. The sentiment of our local people is stronger than ever across the state. Some say, Sabah is continuingly receiving[12] a big number of foreigners, despite of the on going repatriation excise for the illegal migrants from Southern Philippines and Indonesia.

The citizenship qualification is spelt out in the Federal Constitution under Part III, sections 14 of Citizenship Rules 1964, which reads:

a. Every person born before Malaysia Day

b. Every person on or after Malaysia Day, and having any of the qualification specified in Part II of the Second Schedule.

Others like Pakistanis and Indians of lately are seen increasing in numbers. The numbers alone could not be made controversial but if local opportunities were jeopardized because of their presence I would say no reason for not questioning the relevant authorities as to how it could happen.

---

11. Most local feel uncomfortable with the large presence of foreigners as indicated in our random interview.

12. Most people interviewed thought so.

Since the aftermath of kidnapping, our authorities have been struggling to improve the security image of course it is great but such concerned must go beyond restraining the possible intruders or kidnappers alone.

Those coming without legal document must be stopped at all cost.

We are yet to know of the effectiveness of this monumental project.

At one time the whole DBKK looks like a deserted island. No more tailors found at the Filipino market, no cigarette and medicine vendors around and not many kids selling plastic bags at the wet market.

But, that was only for a short period. Now most people around DBKK feel that situation is back to square one. If one goes around DBKK the number of foreigners is just like as it was.

Judging from that scenario the number of foreigners than must be big, even by continuing sending them back, large numbers to be found around.

The local people think it is bad idea to have too many foreigners because they dared to do business by whatever means, hawking on foot, by bicycle or motorbike, setting up stalls where and when they think money is to be made.

In the past locals considered, such activities were trivial. But now there is a need to get involved because the whole economy of the country is still not as rosy as it sounds after the economy meltdown.

This simple study indicates that this issue is going to be a dominant for many years to come, unless of course, something is done quickly.

My summing up from that interview are two things, one the present of foreigners create fear in the mind of the local people, for examples in commercial sectors like, fish retailing activities or mongering and catching is dominantly controlled by Filipinos.

Recently it was reported in our local paper that the locals find it difficult to anticipate in fish trade and was even threatened.

Whilst, the Indonesians monopoly in food industries, from *pisang goreng* to food stalls and restaurants in the city and towns.

Nowadays they even supply vegetables to towns. They hire small plot of land from local paying nominal fares monthly. A little while later, the whole family would join them from Indonesia.

There have also been an increasing number of Indonesians of Javanese origins in the Sabah KK areas like, Luyang, Likas, Inanam and Putatan.

I was informed some only arrived recently but managed to obtain trading license to operate business or another example, an Indonesian employed as a religious teacher who arrived only recently has contractor license[13] (to operate a canteen) and the Timorese could get a driving license as 'easy as buying pisang goreng'.

In one of the newly opened restaurants, I heard a strange dialect, I asked whether he is the owner, and if he is why he did not hang the trading license on the wall.

He replied he would do it tomorrow. I have passed many times now I still do not see the trading license.

I consider the fear of the Sabah's future economy overtaken by foreigners is real.

Fear of personal and safety of property is another.

Question hangs at the back of our people's mind is, will the relevant authorities able to reduce the number?

If we read in our local paper nearly 90 percent of killing, properties damaging and fish bombing carried by foreigners so also social ills like drug taking, pushing, thieving and mugging.

Nowadays not many local women dare to wear jewelry's when passing the big market of Kota Kinabalu because of the rampant snatching, just like very few house owners dare to have their houses bare without putting iron grilles.

Keningau is another example. It is linked with the East Coast by Kalabakan highway.

This is the golden passage in as far as the Indonesians from Celebes are concerned. One would see now who dominate food stalls, fish mongering and *tamus*.

I do not see there has been a regular patrolling taken place along this road by authorities.

The illegal immigrants are equally good at hide and seek.

You and me would not be able to differentiate whether they are local or not trough complexion alone except that their dialect.

Even that nowadays they are well rehearsed long before arriving in the Sabah.

Over the years the number of killing among the Bugis community has been increasing.

Police identified for example the use of Bugis knives found in murder cases in several occasions.

The current trend of foreigners that come to the state is different than the earlier ones.

For example, the massive exodus of foreigners in the early 70s was because of the civil war in Southern Philippines.

---

13.   Or licence to operate canteen

They therefore fall under the status of refugees under the definition of UNHCR—UN auspices.

But now the almost all Southern Philippines islands are within the purview of the Muslim Autonomous Government of Southern Philippines lead by Nur Misuari, issue refugee is no more relevant.

Both the Malaysian and Philippines government likewise should seek to settle the issue.

Another problem besides the naiveté of the locals, I would say is to get rid of corruption habit.

It is only too obvious that without the assistant of officials in the relevant authorities these activities could not be so rampant.

16. SABAH'S TRAFFIC TOLL HORRIBLE

29 October 2000

MOST of us have witnessed motor vehicle accidents in one form or the other-from petty ones to those involving deaths.

A few years ago I received one of the most horrifying and gruesome pictures via e-mail, one of the Karak Highway accidents. That lorry driver did not realize until much later, some human flash were hooked to the lower part of his ten-tone lorry, whilst the intestines scattered all over the road. It was a shocking scene.

My daughter asked me then whether the family of the victim could take legal action against the photographer, before even asked me about bringing an action against the lorry driver. I said yes, but depend on the purpose of the photograph really. She has now completed her law degree and I leave it to her to think about it.

In Kota Kinabalu alone, an average of 2089 accidents[14] occurred last year that is about 7 accidents per day. In Sabah, by motorcar accidents contributed the highest figure—an average of 5065.5 a year, followed by lorry 1343.5, by motorcycles 825.5 and by van/buses 816.5.

Going by location topping the list is KK-Kota Kinabalu City 2060.5, Tawau 859, Sandakan 789, Penampang 695 and surprisingly high for its size is Labuan Federal Territory, 367.5.

How much different is it driving in Malaysian compare to other countries that have lower accidents rate? A friend[15] of mine says, "I have been in England for

---

14.   Statistics were obtained from the Department of Police Traffic, Kepayan-1999-2000

seven years and I had not seen any major accident on the road during that period, unlike ours which occurs every day"

It has been frequently said that, if one can drive in KL, one can drive any way in the world. I am not sure what it means, I think, it could mean that we are notorious drivers or else, very good drivers.

I find driving in Kuala Lumpur is much more hectic and frustrating and I notice that the drivers here are among the least courteous in the world. It has also been said that among the contributing factors that caused difficulty in driving is the rush-rush situation. Every body seems to have shorter hours in a day. Every one is in hurry. Overtaking is a way of conserving time and an order of the day. If you do not overtake, others would. So, it is always a kind of *competition* on the road.

We also know that in case of KL-Kuala Lumpur is getting over crowded, the number of vehicles on the road is increasing every minute, whilst, space remain the same.

Driving is, therefore, no longer fun but rather a stressful. It becomes a source of agitation. Thus, human behaviour changes from being a beauty to a beast.

Whilst driving in Kota Kinabalu or Kuching is not as tight as KL, yet no less hectic and annoying, the accident figure is incredibly high.

But the argument above still do not answer the question as to why Malaysia has such a high rate of motor vehicle accidents. Whilst, countries like UK, France, Holland, USA and Australia which cities are more congested have lower accident rate.

On thing I would say is, nearly a quarter[16] of our drivers on the road are inconsiderate and impolite. This one-quarter, once they are behind the wheel, defies any existence of traffic rules and regulations. They were no more *bersopan*. This one-quarter may also include those who have just passed driving test and owned *flying licenses*.

I am not questioning of whether they are competent drivers or not, with the exception of small percentage, of course.

The issue is about the attitude of mind. Though it has been well written in the Highway Code Part II & I, I wonder how many bother reading it, if the instructor does not let alone the student. Those three-quarters again have very little consciousness, consideration and tolerance toward other drivers and road users.

---

15. Experienced by some former students, who stayed in England and some parts of Europe, including the writer?
16. Only my observation, there has been no statistics or study conducted.

They overtake you as they please from left to right or verse visa. Overtaking from left is only permissible under Rule 5(a) of Road Traffic Rules, 1959l where the driver having indicated an intention to turn right has drawn to the centre of the road...

Making turn or U-turns without giving signal or giving ample time for other drivers to see is another common phenomena contributes to the high incident of accident on the road. Driving very fast or very slowly at the wrong place or at the wrong time without giving proper indication is all too common. Although there is no mention, that driving slowly is against the rule.

The Rule 4 under Road Traffic Rules, 1959 states, "Every vehicle, which is being driven at a slow speed, shall be driven as close to the left hand side of the road.... In such manner as not to obstruct others..." but obviously if it is too slow this could be construed as obstruction which falls Rule 16 (a) of the Act, which says, no driver in charge of a vehicle shall cause or permit the vehicle to stand on a road as to cause any unnecessary obstruction...

Some mini bus drivers are among the worst of all. Just watch how they behave in the city like KK.

Many of the mini buses have this writing "Bas Berhenti-Henti", which impliedly to tell public that they could stop wherever and whenever they like.

It has no legal connotation to this writing whatsoever.

I once asked a high-ranking Sabah JPJ official why such slogans have been allowed. He blames Puspakom for not ensuring that the phrase is removed during the check ups.

Obviously, if true, either JPJ-Jabatan Pengangkutan Jalan or Puspakom-licensing department is not doing what they are supposed to do.

Stopping at an undesignated route for loading or unloading is another common sight in KK, for example at the junction in Lido area whilst the actual bus stop is just about twenty to thirty yards away.

Strangely, hardly any traffic cops can be seen here. They much prefer checking road tax and drivers licenses.

I suggest that public transport like mini buses have one colour as identification like the school buses, so that it could easily identified by passenger and tourist alike.

The JPJ and the driving school in the country must take a hard look at improving the conduct of drivers on the wheel that must begin during the training period. And that good attitude of mind is prerequisite to passing the driving test.

Driving instructors must be able to communicate effectively to inculcate good behaviour. It does not matter what language as long as the massage is conveyed and understood by new driver.

The quality of driving on commercial vehicle like tankers and big lorries presently is not of high standard. Very often, we see in the highway that lorries and tanker exceed the speed limit of 90 km per hour.

A simple check-up on the road will also reveal about two fifths of the drivers to be the Bugis and Timorese, who according to some, got the licenses to drive as easy as buying bananas.

Some had just arrived in this country as short as three months managed to get a class D license.

I therefore find it difficult to believe when the local JPJ Director[17] said Sabah is clean from flying licenses.

To me if fake birth certificate and identity cards are plentiful, making licenses is no more difficult.

I came cross one person[18] who desperately wanted to renew his road tax for a lorry and I know for sure that he could not do it because someone else has the original registration card to my surprise he did it in minutes.

Lorries park at night on the hard shoulder is another common sight for examples, Bukit Padang to the Reservoir Garden and Golf View residential areas.

17. ABU SAYYAF AND OTHER ILLEGAL ACTIVITIES

1 October 2000

ABOUT three months ago I wrote in this column about the likelihood of a second kidnapping in Sabah. I identified cursorily a few islands in the East Coast, which are vulnerable to ransacking and kidnapping by the bandits like Abu Sayyaf.

Something has to be done quickly and concretely to avoid the reoccurring of the Sipadan incident. To me, a Ministers' responsibilities should be more than just giving press conference after press conference.

---

17.   Malaysia TV3
18.   The writer knew him personally.

I still recall one[19] of the Federal Ministers said that the Sipadan kidnapping last April was an isolated case.

He advised the public not to be unduly worried.

I am writing again here, after being proven right, not specifically to prove that the Minister was wrong. I want to emphasize that security matter in this area had not seemed a priority until the last two incidents happened.

Only after the Sipadan kidnapping were we told that a naval base is to be built in Semporna. Only after Pandanan Island incident did we hear that the authority decided on a shoot on sight policy.

The security problem has been left far too long, as if we are condoning the presence of illegal immigrants doing illegal[20] activities in Sabah.

Because of the leniency, Malaysian was even accused of providing military training for Filipinos Muslims by some quarters.

Ex-state Secretary Tan Sri Richard Lind did make his points recently in the Daily Express, when he said business people involved in tourism industry should weigh matters related to security and not rely on the government alone to provide security protection.

He is correct, up to a point. But to what extend, would the business people involve with the security preparations?

Obviously, the normal security guards like some of those we used to see in Kota Kinabalu will not do. Not only do they look fragile and untrained-they are surely no match for the Abu Sayyaf who are equipped and are engaged in "practical training" with the Philippine army in life or death encounter daily.

On top of that, how many of our local companies prepared to invest on security personals as well as equipment? This allocation is entirely new in their budget.

Or must a company own an *army-like* set up to counter the problem of hostage taking or ransacking?

I think, for countering the *bandits* and other illegal activities is would be better to leave it to the authority. Otherwise, we have to create another law allowing the resort operators to own weapons.

The tourism industry is about attracting tourists from abroad. If I were a tourist, I would prefer a place where I could feel relax in mind as well as body.

Surely, I will not feel comfortable being watched by security personals or being guarded by security system alike.

---

19. Deputy Minister of Defense, Datuk Shaffie Afdal
20. Among illegal activities are smuggling items, fish bombing, etc.

Sabah would not be my first choice for holiday destination.

Thus, by stationing heavy security on these tourists' spots, we are chasing the tourists out rather than inviting them in. Whilst, leaving it as it were, is like expecting *a time bomb*. We are caught between the devil and the deep blue sea.

I think we have no choice; there is an urgent and dire need to have a tight planned and controlled situation of our coastal, seas and ports. The idea is not only to deter Abu Sayyaf but also other illegal activities that have been around for a very long time.

Let's forget Sipadan and Pandanan for a while. What about Labuan Island, which is far from Jolo the bandits' home ground?

Our enforces are not doing their job[21] based on the number of cigarettes and alcoholic drink sellers swelling in towns and city, favourite occupation for the immigrants.

Are some among our marine police and customs closing their eyes to the passing smugglers?

And often only the small fry [usually the lorry driver] is caught whilst the *bosses* are running loose.

The most vulnerable coastal area is about 400km long, which must be zoomed into, according to observation by those who are familiar with the area.

No easy way to handle the *lanun* once landed in our territory, they look like local, and they could speak like local. As Commander Robot was saying that he had been to Sabah and many relatives here. That is not surprising at all.

I met a man in Kotabato, Davao, and a few years ago who confessed that he was once a pirate. Whenever he was in Sabah waters he used to shoot the lighthouse. I did feel eerie setting beside to him.

Besides, the Filipinos, the Indonesians are the next largest group of foreigners. The authority should be watching closely, if lately their number had also increasing.

They have not done any physical kidnapping yet but can "kidnap" local *rights* like, getting *flying* licences for taxi, for driving mini buses and licenses for petty traders, restaurants and food stalls.

Many locals complain of not getting those licenses that easily. Yet the newly-arrived Indonesians could easily get them.

---

21. A man from Pulau Gaya used to tell me that the authority harassed his sister for selling a few packs of cigarettes. He also knew and saw the enforcement officers behind and connected to this *trade*.

"Check our taxi stands in towns who are the drivers, and who drive our lorries and tankers," said Abdul, a local taxi driver[22] on afternoon.

Of course, among other arguments, the locals are accused for not wanting these jobs. But I think that is unjustified statement because many of our people are unemployed[23] and many may not know how to go about job prospects unless assisted or informed.

I have no complaint on stationing our arm forces on the strategic locations. It should have been done long time ago.

They must be equipped with devices so that detection can be made easily. The authority must be prepared to invest on equipment and the rest.

It is important to have a joint border watch on seas, on land, immigration, and marine activities with the Philippines government and the Indonesians governments.

A political solution on issue of Philippines claim over Sarah has to be initiated and be put into rest because Sabahans are happy as they are now in Malaysia.

It is irony that many Malaysians do not even know the background of the claim, let alone to participate in the debate.

On the matter of security again, I find it very strange that only now that the CM is to write[24] to the federal Government asking for extra security assistant.

Was the Government is still in the dark about security after nearly thirty-seven years?

No wonder it took only four Abu Sayyaf to hurt the pride of the Malaysian defence.

The majority of Malaysians would agree with the shoot on sight policy provided it must be consistent.

If no harsh measure is taken, the kidnapping activity is here to stay and may be next, the Abu Sayyaf would target individuals or prominent people, operating like Mafiosi.

Hostage taking is lucrative business imagine, 1 million pesos per head (RM 333,000.00), and not surprising the Abu Sayyaf used 750 horsepower engine vessel. They may even be able to afford a few by now.

Abu Sayyaf is not fighting for political course.

They are after money, contrary to what they claim.

---

22.   This is not the real name but I talked to the person.
23.   Being naïve in nature, they do not know how to go about unless assisted and informed.
24.   Chief Minister's statement appeared in the local media recently

Fighting a political course is not targeted at individual, but rather authority or military in this respect.

I recalled an article during the early days of Sipadan hostage crisis, where the writer pointed out that most males in Jolo are jobless and lazy. It is the females normally the breadwinners.

Males like cock fighting, fighting among them, terrorizing and kidnapping people. And they are proud of having many wives.

I am also curious why the Governor of Muslim Autonomous Region—Nur Masuari was not taking an active part to help solve this kidnapping crisis.

I thought a person of great experience and a rebel leader at one time could be able to provide tips to deal with *his* people.

We are paying a heavy price indeed for allowing the relatives of Abu Sayyaf to vote in our state and parliamentary general election through our own carelessness or stupidity.

So, it is only natural for some of them to assume if they could vote in elections, by right there is no reason for us to shoot them on sight in return.

Make his points recently in the Daily Express, when he said business people involved in tourism industry should weigh matters related to security and not rely on the government alone to provide security protection.

He is correct, up to a point. But to what extend, would the business people involve with the security preparations?

Obviously, the normal security guards like some of those we used to see in Kota Kinabalu will not do. Not only do they look fragile and untrained-they are surely no match for the Abu Sayyaf who are equipped and are engaged in "practical training" with the Philippine army in life or death encounter daily.

On top of that, how many of our local companies prepared to invest on security personals as well as equipment? This allocation is entirely new in their budget.

Or must a company own an *army-like* set up to counter the problem of hostage taking or ransacking?

I think, for countering the *bandits* and other illegal activities is would be better to leave it to the authority. Otherwise, we have to create another law allowing the resort operators to own weapons.

The tourism industry is about attracting tourists from abroad. If I were a tourist, I would prefer a place where I could feel relax in mind as well as body.

Surely, I will not feel comfortable being watched by security personals or being guarded by security system alike.

Sabah would not be my first choice for holiday destination.

Thus, by stationing heavy security on these tourists' spots, we are chasing the tourists out rather than inviting them in. Whilst, leaving it as it were, is like expecting *a time bomb*. We are caught between the devil and the deep blue sea.

I think we have no choice; there is an urgent and dire need to have a tight planned and controlled situation of our coastal, seas and ports. The idea is not only to deter Abu Sayyaf but also other illegal activities that have been around for a very long time.

Let's forget Sipadan and Pandanan for a while. What about Labuan Island? Which is far from Jolo, the bandits' home ground.

Our enforces are not doing their job[25] based on the number of cigarettes and alcoholic drink sellers swelling in towns and city, favourite occupation for the immigrants.

Are some among our marine police and customs closing their eyes to the passing smugglers?

And often only the small fry [usually the lorry driver] is caught whilst the *bosses* are running loose.

The most vulnerable coastal area is about 400km long, which must be zoomed into, according to observation by those who are familiar with the area.

No easy way to handle the *lanun* once landed in our territory, they look like local, and they could speak like local. As Commander Robot was saying that he had been to Sabah and many relatives here. That is not surprising at all.

I met a man in Kotabato, Davao, and a few years ago who confessed that he was once a pirate. Whenever he was in Sabah waters he used to shoot the lighthouse. I did feel eerie setting beside to him.

Besides, the Filipinos, the Indonesians are the next largest group of foreigners. The authority should be watching closely, if lately their number had also increasing.

They have not done any physical kidnapping yet but can "kidnap" local *rights* like, getting *flying* licences for taxi, for driving mini buses and licences for petty traders, restaurants and food stalls.

Many locals complain of not getting those licences that easily. Yet the newly-arrived Indonesians could easily get them.

"Check our taxi stands in towns who are the drivers, and who drive our lorries and tankers," said Abdul, a local taxi driver[26] on afternoon.

---

25. A man from Pulau Gaya used to tell me that the authority harassed his sister for selling a few packs of cigarettes. He also knew and saw the enforcement officers behind and connected to this *trade*.

26. This is not the real name but I talked to the person.

Of course, among other arguments, the locals are accused for not wanting these jobs. But I think that is unjustified statement because many of our people are unemployed[27] and many may not know how to go about job prospects unless assisted or informed.

I have no complaint on stationing our arm forces on the strategic locations. It should have been done long time ago.

They must be equipped with devices so that detection can be made easily. The authority must be prepared to invest on equipment and the rest.

It is important to have a joint border watch on seas, on land, immigration, and marine activities with the Philippines government and the Indonesians governments.

A political solution on issue of Philippines claim over Sabah has to be initiated and be put into rest because Sabahans are happy as they are now in Malaysia.

It is irony that many Malaysians do not even know the background of the claim, let alone to participate in the debate.

On the matter of security again, I find it very strange that only now that the CM is to write[28] to the federal Government asking for extra security assistant.

Was the Government is still in the dark about security after nearly thirty-seven years?

No wonder it took only four Abu Sayyaf to hurt the pride of the Malaysian defence.

The majority of Malaysians would agree with the shoot on sight policy provided it must be consistent.

If no harsh measure is taken, the kidnapping activity is here to stay and may be next, the Abu Sayyaf would target individuals or prominent people, operating like Mafiosi.

Hostage taking is lucrative business imagine, 1 million pesos per head (RM 333,000.00), and not surprising the Abu Sayyaf used 750 horsepower engine vessel. They may even be able to afford a few by now.

Abu Sayyaf is not fighting for political course.

They are after money, contrary to what they claim.

Fighting a political course is not targeted at individual, but rather authority or military in this respect.

---

27. Being naïve in nature, they do not know how to go about unless assisted and informed.
28. Chief Minister's statement appeared in the local media recently

I recalled an article during the early days of Sipadan hostage crisis, where the writer pointed out that most males in Jolo are jobless and lazy. It is the females normally the breadwinners.

Males like cock fighting, fighting among them, terrorizing and kidnapping people. And they are proud of having many wives.

I am also curious why the Governor of Muslim Autonomous Region—Nur Masuari was not taking an active part to help solve this kidnapping crisis.

I thought a person of great experience and a rebel leader at one time could be able to provide tips to deal with *his* people.

We are paying a heavy price indeed for allowing the relatives of Abu Sayyaf to vote in our state and parliamentary general election through our own carelessness or stupidity.

So, it is only natural for some of them to assume if they could vote in elections, by right there is no reason for us to shoot them on sight in return.

18. MORE FISH BOMBING

20 August 2000

THE environmental issue is something that must not be taken lightly any more. Concern about it is growing by day whether one likes it or not.

But in our case, we still need plenty of hard work in order to create a greater awareness among our people. At the *kampong* level in Sabah issues of environment have not been taken up seriously.

The *kampong* people never really feel something is greatly *wrong* until the better-informed generation like sons, daughters or grandsons and grand daughters or great-grant sons/daughters start talking about it.

The level of understanding about environmental problems overall is still quite low, more so for matters that is not quite straightforward.

For example, damage of our coral, disappearance of certain species of insects, lack of habitat for wild animal, missing plant, and etc.

Ironically, even the better-informed towns and city dwellers are apt to miss some points on environment these days.

Bombed fish continue to be put on sale at the wet market in Kota Kinabalu right under the nose of enforcement officers like DBKK-City Hall of Kota Kinabalu.

One will be surprised to come across that *ikan putih* would cost only RM3.00 per kilo in Kota Kinabalu wet market, whilst usually it costs RM7.00 or more per kilo.

Surely, something is not quite right with our pricing system, when such fluctuation is so drastic within a month let alone a week.

When I question the sellers why is it cheap, they seldom answer. Or if they do it will be:

"Saya beli dari orang" He or she bought it from someone else.

For the sellers, buying from someone knowingly or unknowingly does not give him or her a 'licence' to sell bombed fish. It is not difficult for those in the trade to guess the fish is bombed.

In fish bombing, the explosives are dropped in the sea or river indiscriminately. This is one of the easiest ways of catching fish in abundance.

Our legal definition on bombed fish under Section 26 of Fisheries Act 1985-*fishing with the use of any explosive, poison or pollutant, or any apparatus utilizing an electric current, or any prohibited gear, for the purpose of killing, stunning, disabling or catching fish, or in any other way rendering such fish more easily caught.*

Any one found to violating this section using or even attempting, carrying or in possession or under one control knowing or having reasonable cause to believe shall be guilty of an offence.

Under Section 25(b) offender is liable to fine for not exceeding to twenty thousand ringgits or a term of imprisonment not exceeding two years or both.

For foreign vessel the fine will not exceed one million, for the owner or master of the vessel whilst in the case of member of the crew each will be liable to fine of one RM 100,000.

But based on records[29] authorities have problem in panellising the culprits under this Section 26. Nearly all those brought to court by the Fisheries Department and the Marine Police were charged under section 26 (1) (c) which states,—*any person who knowing or having reasonable cause to believe that any fish is a prohibited species or has been taken in contravention of the provisions of this Act, receives or is found in possession of such fish.*

I wonder why authorities are relying on this sub section 26 (1) (c) and not (a) or (b) with regard to bombed fish.

---

29.   Rekod kes Jabatan Perikanan Sabah 2000

Reports of Marine police[30] successes in seizing bombed fish; equipments, detonators, boats and other materials have been well recorded. I am not sure whether to congratulate.

What does it mean when seizing is becoming more frequent?

Either the marine police's method of catching the culprits is becoming more effective or else; the number involved in fish bombing is increasing.

Either way, it still indicates bombing is flourishing activity.

No figures show if there is any reduction in numbers of the bombing in the last couples of years. Most of what reported in the media is that the Marine Police were getting bigger and bigger caught in term of the size and varieties.

Most of the extensive bombings in Sabah were and are carried out by illegal immigrants. Recently, it was reported that an ex-marine lost his thumb when a self-made bomb exploded at his premises.

Some Filipinos who happened to be at his house reportedly took him to hospital. Since nothing came out of the case the public to presume that there has been a cover-up by the authority concerned.

Now back to the fish, the appearance of bombed fish is just like any other fish caught by the conventional methods, until one examines very closely.

One would find that, the stomach of the fish is soft, the body is smashed, and the rib bones are broken and easily rot. If kept in the deep freezer for a longer period, some say, the taste is pungent.

As to the side affect, after eating the bombed fish, the Doctor, [medical practitioner] whom I spoke to, said, it depends on what kind of explosives used.

But sometimes these people are resorting to use cyanide, a damned poisonous chemical. It can kill human being if consumed.

The Fisheries Department stated that in the West Coast of Sabah, the concentration of those involved in bombing are those found living near by islands like, Pulau Pondo and Pulau Gaya.

The most popular spots are Mangalum and Mantanani; the nearer ones are like Pulau Tiga, Pulau Gaya, and Malawali at the oil rags in Labuan, Balambangan.

There are few authorities that deal with enforcement of bombed fish for Sabah; the Marine Police, the Fisheries Department and DBKK of course each have different power and jurisdiction.

For those environment conscious, such bombing activities are something cannot be tolerated in today's scenario.

---

30.   Reported in Daily Express on March 15th, 2000

Our next generation will curse us for being irresponsible in letting the quality of our environment go to the dogs.

Have we really taken an effort to better educate ourselves in order to educate our kids or our neighbours' kids, to help sustaining the present quality of our environment?

One does not need to be an *active* environmental activist to do the above.

There are tons and tons of documents readily accessible to any one who wants to educate one-self.

A little bit of understanding the concept of 'costs and benefits' would be good enough.

From simple rubbish burning to more controversial proposals involving mining and forest, everything must be thought out carefully because the impact is permanently going to affect the people and ecosystem.

In the case of fish bombings, such activity is not only destroying the targeted fish but all other marine organisms, including the coral, flora and fauna, which takes many thousand or millions years to form.

The consequence of their doing would, in fact, decease the quality of environment. Because many parts that keep environment sustainable are missing.

Our law has provided penalties for those contravened the law on this matter, but enforcement is something else.

In relation to fish bombing, besides, the Fisheries Act 1985, The Explosive Act 1957 (ACT 207) & Explosive Rules 1923, Section 4 deals directly with the wrongful use of explosives.

Section 2 of the Act prohibits the manufacture, possession or importation of dangerous explosives and upon conviction penalty will be imprisonment for five years, whilst Section 19 of the Act entitles the authority to seize and sale the vessels.

There is provision for rewards to informers if it leads to the conviction of the offender or offenders under Section 19, but so far, our people are not in the habit of informing the authorities for reason only known to them.

Among the greatest hurdles would be how to teach the illegal immigrants partly because of their background and the 'sea gypsies' who have no permanent place to live, hopping from one island to another.

Efforts and campaigns has to be continued and carried out by relevant authorities from time to time to create awareness for our fishermen and public alike.

19. MORE CONCERN ON BASIC NEEDS THAN
FROGGING

11 June 2000

OBVIOUSLY, there is a big different between doing politicking and thinking politically. A Politician lives on politicking as well as thinking politically, and some think less than the others.

The non-politician do not live by politicking but some do think about politics, and some even have greater knowledge about politics, such as with PhDs.

Some say politics is an art of possible; categorically it can either be science, art, or the mixture of both. That is why politicians can do wonders.

Politician's argument is always work under the pretext of common good, that is, for the good of *rakyat* and the country. Some politicians even shed tears when explaining of how much he or she cares about the *rakyat* and the country.

Of course, there are some truths in it, whilst, in many occasions there are also plenty of rubbish. Some politicians are good at parroting and imitating theirs piers but produce no new ideas on his or her own, whilst, some nothing but good at *angkat kaki.*

Yet, survive for many rounds. That is politics.

Next, issue on *'froging'*, a term commonly used in Sabah these days for politicians crossing from one political party to another, especially from the opposition to the ruling government.

For a non-politician, it would be very interesting to listen to YBs' reasons, why they switched political party. Only yesterday, they argued each other like hell and now they sit together in one table agreeing almost everything even if they do not hear what the other is saying. That can happen only in politics.

In politics forget and forgive is the rule of the game, ordinary people or civil servants alike who get entangled so seriously with politician, too often get victimized and fall fry by the other politicians. It happens, because politics has no standard procedures to be followed.

Not many of our politicians fight about ideology or philosophy; we are not yet cultured to do that. Even in the state *dewan*, argument is only done cursorily the speaker does not play a role as referee as such. I can understand that, because he was appointed by the government of the day.

Dr Jeffrey's[31] article "Reconciling the Irreconcilable", must have been eagerly waited by many people. He has put down his reasons for crossing to BN. He pointed out how and what it would be like to stick with the opposition.

That the *rakyat* must be expecting too highly from politicians these days, regardless what political party they are from.

Dr Jeffery explained being a politician he has to do something for the good of the people. He has realized after two years in the wilderness, led him no way. He could not pursue the inspiration by the people being in the opposition camp. His voters would be losing out much by the five-year term ends.

Dr Jeffery realized that he has been parochial all this while, that was not good for Sabah. One must be thinking of the whole Malaysia, because Sabah will go no way by its own, and no room for thinking for our own interests alone.

I would not disagree up to this point; it sounds great because it is for common good.

Some people are sceptical about it though. They see it as an issue of political survival whilst, others consider it as political compromise.

Nonetheless, some think that the five YBs are tired of fighting the losing battle, with no forthcoming rewards. No rewards mean nothing for the voters. Like Malay saying, *'Ayam Menang Kampong Tergadai'*—one wins the cock-fighting competition but has to auction the village.

Life as a YB is no longer easy. He has to keep up with the voters' expectation. In other words, money is difficult to get being in the opposition side. *Kayu balak* is longer accessible to any YB as was thirty or forty years ago. A part from that our younger generation is concerned about the thousands upon thousands of hectors of barren land with no apparent re plantation like on the way to Long Pasia.

Back to issue of crossing over, obviously the five YBs must have calculated the costs and benefits. Let's hope they did it not for self-interest or out of selfishness.

Staying a float is not good enough for them, and for the people. People want development. In Sabah, development means infrastructure, like roads, water supply, and electricity, still the very basic ones including shelters.

One will remember a few years back the former Chief Minister Datuk Yong Teck Lee gave a talk to civil servants at the auditorium of Yayasan Sabah.

Slide shows then showed how bad Rungus' houses were. I visited the place only this year. It has not changed either—see photo provided taken at Kampong Taringai Laut, Kudat.

---

31. Dr Jeffery and the writers know each other.

Looking at the condition of the houses, poverty is not confined to Nabawan as frequently quoted in the media. Equally, it would be a big mistake to say that there is no poverty in Sabah[32]. Whatever economic yardstick is used to determine poverty, I have no doubt poverty[33] exists in Sabah.

If the YBs could address this issue not only their calculation is right but also I think their venture is worthwhile and well support by the people. But if they are wrong, the repercussion is great and they may not be able to march for the next round.

Or I maybe wrong. Based on our political history; this is a normal scenario. Even to date, we still find some of our politicians who survived from the 60s.

Material wealth determines the destiny of political journey. That is why we see the same faces or family connections in every subsequent election.

Also in our case, win means; win all, no half way. If you fight hard from the opposition's side, the whole mechanism will fall against you and not many YBs prepare to fight unless their bank balances are stable or have been given untold acres of land while their party was in power that are now fruiting with oil palm.

To some of us, the increase number of the opposition YBs like PAS in the *Dewan Rakyat* is seen as good development for our political maturity, their existence would help to check and balance, thus the government benches would have less napping hours at the *Dewan*.

Are people at large concerned very much about *froging*? In my view, they are still concerned about meeting their day-to-day needs.

20. SABAH ANOTHER JOLO

25 June 2000

AWAITING judgment from ICJ (International Court of Justice) was reported to be the reason or the cutback in security in Sipadan.

And for this, we have to pay a heavy price.

The Sipadan Island hostage incident has been planned, not by flick of mind. Kan Yaw Chong of Daily Express in his report drew attention to the visibility

---

32. Study of Poverty carried out by the Royal Commission on the Distribution of Income and Wealth in the UK, Peter Townsend, 1979.
33. The writer has involved extensively with the rural people for the last two years. He has visited the entire state, providing health services.

that night like the size of moon and calm waters, among others, that suggested a well-calculated operation.

It is also heartless if it is true that Sabah-based businessman financed the kidnapping.

The decision for not keeping a close watch on this island was terribly flawed.

Whether the authority did or did not 'guard' the island it bears little impact on the ICJ Court's ruling.

Malaysians[34] of Sabah origin have been in this island for more than hundred years ago.

There must be no lax in security either for other tourist spots like Mabul Island and Sipalai Island.

Attack or ransacking by pirates, are not unexpected here, since most of Malaysian's islands on the East Coast of Sabah are on the open high sea. The issue of insecurity is not new; the choice is rather on the pirates—when to strike or not to strike.

A string of attacks has taken place even at town center of Semporna in the last few years.

Sometimes armed pirates with machine guns used cars to chase their victims in the mainland.

A year ago a Yayasan Sabah driver was chased while driving from Lahad Datu to Tawau to pick up his boss at Tawau airport in the early morning.

"Luckily it was a brand new Pajero, I could not press the accelerator any more. I don't know what they were after. They must have thought I am a rich man because of the new car," said the driver named Steven.

Many fishermen said that the pirates have always been active in this area, some incidents were reported to the authorities and some were not.

What the locals expect in places like Semporna are extra security measures.

The Malaysian security forces must be well equipped. The pirates' boats are said to be faster including those of the Philippine Marines.

In 48 months'[35] Semporna will have its first permanent naval based-37 years after Sabah gained its independent through Malaysia.

The porosity of the border between the Philippines and Sabah-Malaysia is obviously makes it impossible to have watertight boarder control.

---

34. Continuous occupancy as this, and effective control are among the strong points for recognition of ownership under the International law.

35. According to Malaysian Government Minister, reported in Daily Express on May 3, 2000

The inhabitants of the Southern Philippines islands were and still are at war with their government for as long as we can remember. The problem is not new.

Of course deporting all is an impossible task. These people keep on coming back.

But again, should we not do anything, Sabah could well be another Jolo?

We have enough social problem created by these illegal immigrants, ranging from drug pushing, and abuse to pick pocketing, robbing and other menaces too many to mention.

Innocent citizens feel insecure unlike the Sabah that was 30 or 50 years ago.

Yet the Abu Sayyaf said, Malaysian authority is treating the Bangsamoro badly.

Based on what I have seen, Malaysia has given the illegal immigrants much better treatment. than most developed countries.

The State government has spent a great deal of money in keeping these people, monitoring them and maintaining them while on transit before deporting to their home countries.

They are said to enjoy a menu of chicken or beef once a week while pending deportation. Transportation to deportation point is via air-con coaches.

These people fill up majority of Sabah's lock-ups.

Cigarettes sold illegally and Syabu and other drug as well as fire are in the increase. Their squatter colonies have yielded weapons with which they have attacked our enforcement personnel and even killed some of them.

We support the authority's doing, except that, the efforts should have come much earlier and not when the when the troubles almost reached the neck, so to speak.

One Minister commented that, some years ago extra security personnel were stationed on the islands, but because of tourism it was decided not to continue such policy.

I find the reason is very unconvincing.

A housewife in Semporna told me her house was robbed many times and in one occasion even the empty gas tank was taken away. Now she has no more ideas where to keep her valuables.

Both the Malaysia government and Philippines government have to consider several pertinent issues in order reduce this serious problem:

- Both governments must have a proper arrangement or mechanism to deal with security on the boarder. Priority is to ensure people and property is safe. Take account that Sabah has long open coastal line.

- The Philippine government must once and for all not drop its claim over Sabah. A permanent political solution must be found no matter how tricky the subject is.

Malaysia has business interest in Sipadan Island, and I see no reason why no extra precaution was taken place.

I am not suggesting that, platoons of army or fleets of marine police be to be stationed on the island.

But the island should have been closely watched to deter the possible intrusion.

Malaysia is duty bound to make sure that her citizens are safe, I have no doubt that international law recognizes who has better right under such circumstances.

The "Suluk connection" in Sabah's history does not give rights for Abu Sayyaf to take hostage as bargaining chip just because of history.

Nor does Islamic advocates to fight in the manner they do either.

It is unethical to use religious as a fall back when the fight is for something else.

Because of Sipadan incident, the whole world knows not just where Sabah is but also that Sabah has a huge illegal immigrant problems comprising Filipinos from many parts of Philippines, Indonesian especially from Celebes followed by the Timorese from Flores.

The number of illegal immigrants found in Peninsula Malaysia is not even quarter of what Sabah has.

They were not only visible for a long time but lately become audible with bangs in the night.

21. HOSTING *KAAMATAN*

28 May, 2000

I FIND it interesting to see that so many of ethnic association leaders sit together for the first time and prepare this year's *Pest Kaamatan*.

In other words, the *Pesta Kaamatan* is no longer viewed as Kadazan/Dusun 'sole proprietary' as such, but very much belong to all Sabahans and Malaysians, in general.

Traditionally, the Kadazan/Dusun and Murut spearheaded the celebration. But this time around the *Sabah Momogon Rungus Association* (SMOA) has been given the honor to host it.

The decision to rotate the hosting has caught some of the associations' leaders by surprise.

The idea behind it is to enable other ethnic-cultural associations to host the celebration. Except, I do not see how the concept of rotation can really be justified.

I do not agree if it's just for the sake of rotation. Or it is to give a political mileage to some association leaders.

Take for example, a small association like *Persatuan Kedayan Sabah* (KEDAYAN) or *Persatuan Iranun.*

It is not an issue of competency or capability to host. We have to be practical and try to understand the very objectives of the festival. Otherwise, it defeats the whole purpose of celebration.

Therefore, participating as a team is still the best method for the good of a whole.

In my view is that, the Kadazan/Dusun must still be playing a major role as well as be given an upper hand in making the celebration alive, while the government of the day gives guidance.

My personal experience as a leader of an association of ethnic origin for many years is this-participate in making the respective associations active first.

The objectives of any ethnic associations are nearly similar, i.e. to assist members to create awareness of 'the surroundings' vis-a vis education, social, welfare, political, economics, religions and, etc.

To do that, the executives of the associations have to visit the branches in various *kampongs,* conduct meetings and hold many discussions at the branch level.

To carry out such activities require a lot of energy, money, time and many more.

In doing so a large section of community could often misinterpret the motives unless they are properly informed, they think these activities are another form of politicking.

The politicians in one hand can get easily envious. That is why some politicians head ethnic associations.

Finance is the single most important factor that determines the survival or active-ness of any association.

So a small ethnic association, which has large membership but where fees are not even charged, surely fined it difficult to be self-financed. That is why only the associations headed by politicians are likely to be moving energetically.

Any other associations headed by a person with no 'political title' would find it hard, despite the fact that the true intention and interest is to help their members.

Come back to the *Kaamatan* issue, there has been talked about reviewing the *Kaamatan Festival.* Politicians say the move is to get rid the negative aspects of the celebration, I have not got the clue what the politicians are talking about.

Another is to make the *Kaamatan celebration* as national celebration. This deserves support.

As mentioned earlier, this years' *Pesta Kamaatan* is different from previous because twelve other ethnic-indigenous associations invited to participate in the celebration besides *Kadazan Dusun Cultural Association* (KDCA) and *Persatuan Sabah Murut Bersatu* (PSMB) are:

Persatuan Momogon Rungus Sabah (SAMORA), *Persatuan Seni Budaya Bajau Sabah* (PSBB), *United Sabah Dusun Association* (USDA), *Persatuan Masyarakat Brunei Sabah* (PMBS), *Persatuan Bisaya Bersatu Sabah* (PBBS), *Persatuan Bangsa Sungai Sabah* (SABAS), *Persatuan Bumiputra Iranun Sabah* (PISBA), *Persatuan Keadayan Sabah* (KEDAYAN), *Persatuan Kebudayan Lundayeh Sabah* (PKLS), *Persatuan Tabilong Bersatu Sabah* (PTBS), *Persatuan Masyarakat Gaana Sabah* (PMGS), *Persatuan Tidong Sabah* (PTS) and *Persatuan Kebajikan Bugis Sabah*(PKBS)

There are two things in the organizers' mind by inviting all ethnic associations come together, one, is to strengthen the existing *perpaduan*, second, and to woe foreign tourists coincides with the Visit Sabah Year 2000.

Such combined efforts like this should be encouraged, and Sabah has abundant of cultural diversities and charm, colourful traditional dresses, varieties of traditional games to be displayed during the celebration which surely, enough to incite and excite visitors.

The last year's celebration created a little bit of confusion, because the State and the KDCA held two separate Kaamatans.

Ask mentioned earlier, almost all ethnic association were invited this year for the first time. This is recognition to them, which has never occurred before. I would think this is a healthy development.

I always believed it would be unreasonable to dismiss their existence. They are part of the whole in the making up our society and there is no good reason to isolate them.

I have come across several times, when friends argued that having *Persatuan Bangsa* (race based associations) could create fractions, my argument is, and no body can get rid of the race element. It is fact of life.

We have seen what has happened in Kosovo and many parts of the world that isolating ethnic groupings as bad as ethnic cleansing.

In Sabah, we have never had problem with races. No untoward incident or history of racial infighting ever occurred because of race.

Politicians do once a while take opportunity to touch on racial issue but none other than for their political mileage.

The *Kaamaatan* is the celebration of cultural and ritual of Kadazan and Dusuns inherited from their forefathers, from many generations ago to mark the end of harvesting *padi*.

In the beginning it started with a simple celebration. Then they were public holidays and later turned to be a state affair, highlighted throughout the state especially during the PBS government.

We have no quarrel about it, because it falls well within the rule of democracy.

The celebration augured well ever since and is another important treasure of Malaysians.

The preparations for this year celebration are going on smoothly. Everyone is contributing his or her best.

Still, as always in any celebration of this nature the biggest headache for the organizers is financial.

The various ethnic associations is that, are a sample of the true picture of living in a multi-racial society. The uniqueness of our society in particular, and Sabah is the living proof.

22. ILLEGAL LOGGERS EVADE CHECKPOINTS.

7 May 2000

MUCH has been said about illegal logging and timber stealing, and this issue is not new in Sabah. But it becomes more rampant and serious in recent years. It is unstoppable.

The fact that such activities are in the ever increasing. Among reasons are that this *business'* is lucrative, easy money, easy to steal and plenty to steal.

People steal because for the fact that it is easy to steal-is not a good reason. Partly, it is because a lot of thieves around. Holders of concessions find it difficult to watch over such a vast areas, remote and situated at torrential locations. For example, those owned by the State government, Yayasan Sabah, Sabah Forest Industry, Safoda, just to name a few.

Four wheels drives are necessary to do the checking and inspecting but unfortunately, not all areas are accessible by road.

The only better way is by aerial viewing but again this is costly, and dependent on weather condition. The timber thieves are good at timing they do it when they are less watched for example, during long holidays or over the weekends.

Overall, it is management failure to overseas its individual concession. This is what matters. The system of overseeing the area is not good enough and too old fashion. We lacked of modern facilities, techniques and devices to detect the culprits.

The Forest Department, likewise, is not equipped or 'not competent' to combat the latest wave of modern timber *pirates* who use the ever sophisticated methods. Bribery is among the easiest ways to blindfold officials from the very top to the very bottom. Indeed this is a tricky subject and difficult to detect, but it happened.

Talking about stealing, I am referring to those logs and timber stolen from those concessionaires mentioned above as examples; this is the most common situation.

But there are cases where the smaller concessionaires situated next to bigger ones. And because of the close proximity, the smaller ones have strong tendency to take opportunity to pinch.

One good example is when the smaller concessionaires have long finished harvesting their areas but is still to be found around. Can we not say that something is fishy?

The Chief Minister made a statement[36] recently (DE March 9) to re deploy the use of army because of the failure of authorities to enforce the law including the Forest Department.

The public is at large in support to the idea of deploying army after all this is public property we are living in peacetime, why not? The Forest Department should have no reason to fear.

The state government and Yayasan Sabah have lost huge amount of revenue. The CM questioned the authorities; despite of the special unit comprised the Forest Department officials and the police to monitor the situation.

The public is also eager to know what are the reasons given by the Forest Department, according to the CM the Forest Department officials were to be called to give explanation.

Some say stealing could not be stopped all together because most of these concession areas are beyond anybody controls.

---

36. The Chief Minister's statement was reported in the Daily Express on March 9, 2000

Most concession areas are situated in remote places. Such areas formed part in partial of *kampong* for local people.

People have been living in there for generations, partly, dependent on jungle products.

But, since timber sale is lucrative venture and the locals have no individual rights to own nor were they given shares as such. Then what is the better thing to do?

For many years, most timber concessionaires recognized the intricacy and therefore did not bother so much if kampong folks steal two or three logs per month.

This is considered as acceptable.

And for the sake of industrial harmony, some timber concessionaires even established what they called, Community Forestry Program.

One example is, Yayasan Sabah, by providing infrastructure, like roads, help them to survey the area for the purpose of gazetting the area as *kampong*, building them a standard timber houses.

But of course, the local people still go to the jungle to hunt for wild animals for food and other things. What else could they go? It is allowable under the Forest Enactment, 1968, Section 41, for saving of natives' rights.

But much of the provisions in this Enactment are to tighten up control by the authority over forestry and very little consideration is taken as to the fate of indigenous people, like, providing them alternatives to earn proper living.

Of late, stealing has becoming more organized and structured, which looks far beyond the *kampong* folk' norm. The number is a no longer two or three log at one time, as it used to be, but amount to many thousands.

Some say that, without high-powered people[37] behind, the normal *kampong* folks would not be that daring. The simple system is being abused.

There has been talked about the saw-millers being involved. The CM even suggested inspecting the saw-millers.

My view is there would not be willing sellers without any willing buyers.

Who were the people involved? That is not easy to pin point at. Although, logistically, the system used in getting the logs out of the jungle seems simple.

For example, cut the tree, by the use of tractor; take it out to the nearby main road, ready lorry to carry it along where it has to pass through several checkpoints before it finally reaches the pick-up point-the log pond.

---

37. Those with positions for example, politicians, community leaders, civil servants and *taukay* alike

Check points are the main deterrence. For any lorry to pass through everything has to be in order, otherwise no go.

Usually manned either by the Forest Department staff or the concessionaires' personals.

I can say if the responsible people assigned to catch the thieves, and if they really want to catch, they could have caught.

But when and if thieves still manage to pass the checkpoints it must be something else.

23. KOTA KINABALU-MALAYSIA'S NEWEST CITY

9 April 2000

CONCEPTUALLY, Kota Kinabalu as a Tropical Rainforest City sounds great but still very abstract from reality. If I were a foreign tourist, the first thing that would strike my mind would be lots wild life on the move-mouse deer, *payau*, *kijang* and monkeys roaming around the city or they even steal food from the open *gerai*.

It must be fun. I hope people of the future are animals loving people. Not long ago I saw a few kids roaming around the city with *lastik* (catapults, self-made) in their hands. I wonder what they are up to.

Or the city that I imagine must have wonderful landscape. At least it must look like golf course-minus holes of course, because it is dangerous for kids.

Nobody is opposing the elevation of KK from Municipal Council to a city.

After all KK has met the criteria of becoming one. As the former Mayor of KL, Tan Sri Elyas Omar said, it is not so much a matter of meeting qualifications.

Even if the city has only 2,000 people, so long as the city could provide facilities, people could live decently and happily, that's what counts.

So, it must be a nerve-wrecking business for the Mayor. I know he is an experience civil servant-an army background.

A friend of mine told me, that the Mayor (before he was made a Mayor) used to shout to show his displeasure over something that did not please him.

Well, that's his style. Provided it works, who cares? I have no squabbles over his shouting norm. I consider him as an all rounder kind of personality.

To date, the City Hall officials must have been very busy.

They have made tremendous efforts in demolishing illegal squatters in and around the city.

I hope those demolished will remain demolished for sometime, kept clean.

At this juncture, the *wargakota* should be supporting where and when they can.

I suggest there should be program made out for this purpose by the City Hall. A get together—like where the *wargakota* regardless their status could take part.

The Mayor put down three priorities during his tenancy, namely: cleanliness, beautification and security.

It sounds simple and logical.

Having RM50 million allocations a year to start with is peanut. It would not last long. And it would therefore, take a few more years before we can really see and feel the difference between living in the city and municipality.

I would like to recap; the Mayor mentioned in the interview with Daily Express during the inauguration of the KK City that a few cities like Paris in Europe and cities in Argentina and Brazil are his favourite.

Of course, that is his views, but for me those cities are not what I would like to consider as model cities.

For example, Paris is an old city not modern. Too crowded and everything else is squeezed in order to make way for any additional new buildings, except as Tan Sri Elyas pointed out that the roads were designed in such away even tourists are unlikely to get lost.

I agree especially the underground system, which I think much simpler than London's.

For the Latin American cities like Buenos Aires and Brasilia, these are also old cities as those found in Europe.

The buildings were erected very much of a mixture of old and new.

They are not clean and have problems like us with illegal and shanty structures sprouting all over the place resulting from their people migrating from country-side to city as well as illegal immigrants from neighbouring countries.

They have plenty of beggars and children beggars from morning to dawn.

Of all cities, I visited, not that many though, I like Canberra in Australia.

It is very clean with lots of beautiful landscaping and no unnecessary traffic jams.

For the buildings, some people find it exotic to look at the mixture of old and new designed buildings, whilst the less artistically minded ones could not care or less about it. The single most important thing is cleanliness.

My observations of KK City is, so far, if it were to look clean, the first and foremost, are to do away with all jetties that are protruding in front of Hyatt Hotel and all those found along the coastal area stretch up to Tg. Aru.

In other words, there should not be any landing place for any boats right from Likas Bay-Yayasan Sabah to Tg. Aru.

Next, the wet market and other lapidated structures found along the coastal area should be demolished.

And once the coastal area is tidied, it is necessary also to clean the coast of Pulau Gaya that is facing KK City, otherwise this is going to be a forever an eye sore.

Pulau Gaya should not be made as a place for quarantining illegal.

It should be beautified as part of KK City.

In order to make KK City is a city of its own it must have originality. Among them are naming our streets, roads and residential areas with local names or names that have local flavour; this is not exclusively to KK City but all over the state.

Because what we see now many of the residential areas and buildings are named with very foreign names.

My mother can not tell my auntie where my younger brother stays because she could not pronounce the name of the place properly and because the name is too Americanised like, Beverly Hill, Colonnade, GraceVille, Fairways and so on.

There is no law restricting developers to use such names but if YBs must speak Bahasa Malaysia in the Dewan Rakyat why can this not be extended to public places.

I hope the authority in position to do something should to do it for the common good.

24. ROLE OF ACA—TOO MUCH CORRUPTION

5 March 2000

WHEN the disease AIDS was first discovered and that it had no cure, the piece of news was enough to strike horror for life in human minds. Corruption is a form of disease that can be cured but never get cured. Some say it is worst than aid.

Day in day out we hear our leaders giving advice to civil servants, politicians and general public alike—"stay away from graft and remain non-partisan".

Of course, many have been caught whilst many more on the loose and many more perhaps do not realize their doings are of an offence in the eyes of law.

During both the state and parliamentary election campaign last year, we heard loud and clear about the accusations and counter accusations by politicians about corruption, who corrupted leaders were, and who were not. At the end of the day we knew no body is really clean.

Corruption is a universal disease; it happened everywhere, every day and it takes many forms. Some are very obvious, some are less, and some are too technical to be understood.

Generally, people have a general idea what corruption is. And one thing for sure, no body likes to be called as 'corrupted person'.

Most definitions we found in the dictionary are less than specific. It depends what one is looking for. I can only sum up, the word corrupt is something equivalent-dishonest.

In our local context-Malaysia, the word corruption does not carry much weight, or is it so? We are a religious and cultural conscious people by virtue of our Asian tradition. We subscribed to living with honesty. Yet corrupt practices occur.

For my purpose in this article, I have to use legal definition cursorily—ACA-The Anti-Corruption Act 1997(ACT 575), in order to provide instant meaning. At the same time we must not forget that legal definition is not unlimited in their usage.

Different places (countries) different people or different time could make definition differ. One can be called a corrupted person in one country but less so in another.

In some parts of Europe, or even in our country it is only normal to find people giving tips to others for providing little service. For example, carrying one's bag to a hotel room or paying a little money to a taxi driver or paying a few centimes to *madam peepee*[38] in the city of Paris for using public toilet—this is not in the case of toilets in Kota Kinabalu.

In some parts of the world, such practice could be construed as bribery; the argument is an employed person is already paid to do the job and should not be paid again.

Or could it be because the amount is much smaller? Mind you, if the client is tycoon from Middle East-some years ago, one could receive a handsome token for carrying his or her luggage to his or her room.

---

38.   This term is in French, a name given to some one who looks after the cleanliness of public toilet in the city of Paris

Our law on Anti—Corruption Act (ACT 575) Part III, Sections 10 up to 20 contained substantial activities which could fall under the definition of corrupt practices. From a simply receiving gratification direct or indirect, carried out or not carried out to a mere intention to mislead could amount to corruption.

It is equally an offence for a person in position to know by virtue of his or her office or position for not reporting any graft activities to the Agency-as required by Section 17.

Activities as we know in law are not exclusively about money or material things; doing or not doing any act could also be interpreted as corrupt practices.

But strangely enough, one is only corrupted when 'caught' and proven guilty by the court of law, those are not detected would escape prosecution, could it mean they are clean?

Adhering to our legal definition could mean thousands of people doing corrupt practices consciously or unconsciously every minute.

This is no easy task for ACA. Proving every case is a tedious job—easier to say than done.

The law covers such a wide area that could be considered an offence and yet it is hard even to catch one.

We are ever worried as to whether a public agency like ACA could performed its task effectively without due influence by men with power. Of course, in all fairness to ACA, it has performed a good job.

ACA must not only intend to be independent but must also be seen to be one. Very often general public tends to think that ACA would only be responsive if instructions are from those in power-a kind of selective prosecution or witch-hunting.

There is no question on being nosy, under the provision of Section 8 of the Act. It is the duty of the Agency to detect any suspect; the Agency cannot just rely on report it receives.

Recent report by Philippine's newspaper said, 50% of the government revenues eats up by corruption the government agencies are the main graft takers. Which means corruption is at the largest in public sectors.

What kind of people is there involved I corruption? They are people at high places—people with influence, power and status in public life, civil servants, and politicians not to mention the 'cronies' and supporters of political masters.

In other words, personal preferences and relationship of blood takes precedence over impersonality.

Fiddling with accounting system and concealing the true picture of the public bodies' financial position is among the commonest ways of hiding from detection.

In China, around 99% are to do with fiddling their profit and loss account. Only last year a mayor was sentenced to 16 years of imprisonment in Beijing and a vice-governor in the central Chinese province of Jiangxi was charged with accepting bribes.

In our context, corruption is more rampant in Government agencies, because these bodies are operating with some degree of autonomy. The idea is, so long as they make money that would be good enough; the executives in power could conceal their guilt.

Some who are not good enough in making profit for the agencies let the agencies go bust[39] we often hear this. Whilst still many of the bosses are no near to be tried for their mistakes.

I would agree with the suggestion that all YBs are to be enforced mandatory compulsory to declare their assets as put forward recently in Parliament this should also include personals who hold top position in public bodies.

Another form of corruption, which happened in broad daylight, is like, distributing zinc, water tanks giving cash, goodies as inducement to vote for a particular person during election time. By definition of our law all these activities are well within corrupt practices.

Many have gone to court since the last few years but so far not many can be cited as good example.

In the course of writing this article I discovered a few things connected to illegal immigrant issue where a community leader[40] in Pulau Gaya was involved in producing counterfeit work permit for illegal immigrants in the state.

Those on the island say this was done in collaboration[41] with people in authority.

In another remote kampong[42] recently, I was told that there were civil servants unwilling even to register local to get their IC without paying money far in excess the actual fees.

Every one knows that there is no levy charged in the making of IC except transportation fares for the journey to the Registration office and ready photos.

---

39. Pawaja Steel could be one of them.
40. It is in Pulau Gaya, a few people prepared to tell the story.
41. Told by the same people as note 3.
42. Salarom in Nabawan, the story was told by the *orang tua kampong* who had experienced it himself

This particular civil servant (name supply to Daily Express) had been so used to receiving money by registering the illegal immigrants at the same time the illegal immigrants were papered to pay any amount unlike our local.

The relevant department must monitor this. There are still quite a number of our local people in remote kampong have not got their birth certificates as well as identity cards.

And if that 'civil servant' I mentioned above are to charge these people for RM300 or more for an identity card, very unlikely for our local people to register themselves.

The ACA, it needs support from various quarters. As we know, our society is not litigious society. Without assurance and well-informed procedures most of them would not like to volunteer.

It is part of the responsibility of the Agency to educate the public under Section 8 of the Act.

25. ABOLISHING-UNHCR STATUS

22 August 1999

SOME people say problems created by illegal immigrants in the state have reached the critical stage. Some may not agree, while others view there is no other solution than sending then home.

James Sarda, in Points to Ponder (DE August 8) asked, whether we have exhausted all our resources in dealing with the illegal.

He said, "No"-the army should be deployed!

This is becoming a tricky subject, some even argue why these people are called illegal not aliens?

The term "illegal immigrants" could be construed as recognizing or accepting their status to stay in this country.

In Europe or in most western countries they prefer to call them alien, meaning citizens of other countries whose rights to stay in a host country are limited.

In Australia,[43] for example, illegal immigrants can be a big local issue even though figuratively the number is only a hundred or so. But we in Sabah are talking about half million or even more of them.

Are we lenient enough and good-hearted people? I think we are.

If there is no interference to our security and privacy to our daily lives, we may not be so aggravated.

The revenge by illegal against the MPKK reinforcement officers has become too much lately.

I support the submission of the Memorandum by the BN components parties recently handed to the Deputy Prime Minister Datuk Abdullah Ahmad Badawi. It should have been done long time ago.

I was once sit in the Task Force Committee of Illegal Immigrants at the early formation of SAPP[44], but after a few meetings the Committee disappeared for no apparent reason.

Much of the discussions in the meetings then were with identifying what the illegal means and comparing the good and the bad of having the illegal immigrants.

Such premises were limited. I felt annoyed because very often when I wanted a particular information from certain government departments the reply would be something like "…that's classified information" I could see this problem was like a time bomb.

I will try to out as to why the illegal immigrants are becoming more daring to the extent of challenging the authorities.

Allegations[45] that illegal were allowed to vote in the state election (Sabah) has been documented and is common knowledge. It means if they have they right to vote they have 'rights', similar to ordinary citizen[46] of the country. It does not matter how the ICs look like, real of fake.

An activity like sending them to their homeland was and is only seen as an ad-hock activity. It has never been seen as serious business.

---

43.   The writer was in Australia in 1998 for about seven months. He observed from reading local papers that illegal immigrants was a serious issue because it involved wastage of public money-though in comparison with Malaysia that the number of illegal immigrants was much less.

44.   Datuk Yong Teck Lee was a close friend of the writer at one time in England. When the writer was the President of Sabah Students' Union of UK and Ireland in 1980, Datuk Yong was the General Secretary of the Union.

45.   Books, Newspapers articles reports and public allegation is all the time

46.   Malaysia, Federal Constitution

Claim over the state of Sabah by the Philippines government has always been viewed as a trade-off. Complicate the matter further.

The State Government seems to have no teeth to press Kuala Lumpur.

Even the most vocal opposition leader will no longer pursue the matter once joining the government side. On top of that, the State government has limited jurisdiction over immigration.

To make matter worse, there was not much action taken during the nine years of PBS rule. It was understandable.

This could be translated that the PBS was hopeless. Good score for BN. But now the ball is with the BN and Sabahans expect a concrete action.

Like any other fields, there have been rampant misuses of position and "corrupt" practices by civil servants and by some people in power, which make things worse. Taking advantage such as hiding them or exploiting them for commercial or political reasons.

The series of articles by Daily Express on the syabu threat facing Sabah some time ago provided an eye opener to many.

About 90% of social problem from syabu and other related on drug abuse to illegal immigrants; recipients were and are our local kids.

Drug abuse leads to other problem like thieving, robbing, snatching, picks pocketing, murder and so on.

The latest double murder of Dr Mahdu Gopal Kulkarni also involved foreigners and whether due to the influence of drugs is yet to be determined by the police.

A single hatred is quite unlikely to lead to such a brutal murder. I knew Kulkarni; I was once sitting in the Committee of Sabah Cancer Society with him some years ago.

He was very loving, caring and unlikely to be not liked by any sensible person.

Another common movie—like activity is snatching jewellery like bracelets and neck chains. They do it in broad day light problems is robbers/thieves enter you car while we are waiting for the traffic light with either knives pointed at you or simply snatch from your neck.

It happened to our staff a few weeks ago, while waiting for the bus to arrive in front of Shell-Parkson Ria in Karamusning.

The onlookers were just speechless. I'm sure many incidents like this are not reported to police.

Another frightening story is a robber who suddenly enters your car and sits next to you while waiting for the traffic light to turn green drawing a knife demanding your wallet or watches or anything valuable.

Make sure your car doors are locked even while travelling as this has happened several times as reported in the Daily Express.

Of course, there is no denying that locals are also involved in these activities, but initially this was not the culture of our society.

Areas such as Lembaga Padi, Sembulan, Bukit Padang must be under constant police monitoring.

What has happened to our beloved State that we suddenly cannot even move freely? We spent a lot of money putting grilles in our houses. Even people in New York or London do not do what we do to our houses.

Another unpleasant sight now is the selling of *ikan tamban* along the coastal high way to Yayasan Sabah. If the authorities do not take action the sight will turn from bad to worse. It is an eyesore.

Let us not be misled by these hawkers as people who experienced buying rotten tam ban to me.

I have no objection to hawking but not in a place like this coast highway, which is too strategic. A Kota Kinabalu landmark is too important to be spoilt. The public must not entertain these hawkers.

Otherwise, this will encourage the to pollute the environment.

Look again at the hawkers selling medicines in Kota Kinabalu, particularly, at the Filipino market. Not only it makes the surrounding ugly, the medicine sold here could also be hazardous to health if taken.

Public agencies and the NGOs should come forward to assist in educating the public and help monitoring these activities.

The public should be made aware of the danger in taking unperceived medicines.

I was once the advisor for the Health Committee of the Unit Hal Ehwal Wanita Sabah and discussed this issue quite at length.

Among the recommendations were that authorities concerned should not let the illegal vendors sell medicine in this manner.

Many local people are still in the habit of buying simple medicine like panadol or aspirins or even cosmetics products, which are mostly fakes.

They are cheaper but people are misled into thinking that these products are all right.

We have underage illegal immigrants kids selling cigarettes all over Sabah and this is not a good way of encouraging people to stop smoking as well as bad for tourism.

Ways and means have to be found to help change public mentality, such consciousness should perhaps be extended to the illegal immigrants community.

Habit of this kind will not go away naturally. Authorities concerned with enforcing the law must devise strategies both short and long-term aims.

I do not see any magical formula to solve these problems.

But to get public confidence, as in law, the authority must not only intend to be serious in dealing with the problems but must also be seen doing it.

The resolution made by one of the BN political parties recently to abolish the status created by UNCHR is another step worth supporting because in doing so it will clarify the true position of the illegal immigrants.

26. SQUATTERS PART OF KOTA KINABALU'S IDENTITY

25 July 1999

SQUATTERS are one of the world's major problems and the numbers are ever increasing. In Malaysia, overall it is still not too bad. But if we pick from State to State basis; the urban squatters in.

Urban Sabah is among the worst. One peculiarity is that urban squatters here are foreigners-mostly-illegal immigrants.

The term illegal immigrant is a person who does not have valid legal document to enter the State like passport and visa that entitles them to stay in this country or work.

These illegal build houses wherever space is available. It makes beautiful surroundings ugly.

In Kota Kinabalu many sites have already been bulldozed.

I may have to borrow the definition of houses or buildings from The Housing Commission Enactment 1967, Section 2 which means to *include house, hut and shed or roofed enclosure*...the houses do not exactly look like houses but merely shelters.

It used to be a common sight in Sabah, for example, today the authority pulled the houses down but no later than tomorrow new houses were erected again on the same spot, the same appearance, and apparently, by the same people. This has been going on like a cat and a mouse game.

Houses like this are easy and cheap to build like the ones at Bukit Nenas and Kampong Mengorok all well within MPKK area. The materials used are cheap and sometimes the tawkays are even prepared to provide free.

In Kota Kinabalu about 80 per cent of houses bulldozed were erected by the illegal immigrants of Filipino origin. The rest 20 per cent is from Indonesia; whilst other foreigners like the Pakistani or Indian, do not build houses at the beginning. They prefer to rent until they could buy one for their own.

The trend is the same in other places especially in the East Coast (Tawau, Sandakan, Lahad Datu, Semporna, Kunak and Kudat).

Now, it has penetrated even into the interior for example Keningau, Ranau and Sipitang.

In Kota Kinabalu, the MPKK zoning area covers within certain kilometre radius, any building to be erected within this area must therefore comply with the new by-law.

In smaller towns in Sabah, there is no imposition by the Ministry of Local Government as to the official specifications of houses or building. The Local Government Act 1976 does not apply in Sabah.

This problem is not new in the State; it started from the early days of post independence or even earlier.

Houses were erected the moment these immigrants arrived because they have nowhere else to stay. Even if accommodations were available, it would be too expensive.

In as far as the Filipinos are concerned; the United Nation accorded the earlier influx (1960s-1970s) a refugee status to these people due to the warfare in Southern Philippines.

Although no time frame was set for the status to be waived, the only common knowledge was that, these people were to be returned to their homeland once the troubles were over.

I wonder how much thought our politicians and administrators had put that time in anticipation of the problems. Should there be strategies developed from the early days, situation could have been different now.

Historical connection with troubled neighbours the Philippines to the north and the poor and overpopulated Sulawesi of Indonesia on the southeast requires a peculiar treatment.

Now the illegal immigrant issue has become so complicated.

So far, all the authority can say is about the numbers of illegal immigrants that had been deported. The numbers on paper might have changed. But seeing every day the reality, that figure does not mean much to the concerned citizens. How do we ensure that illegal housing is not here to stay?

Public sentiment throughout the state is running high now and too important to be ignored by the authorities.

Our local media has been playing a very supportive role in highlighting problems. One cannot miss any news that does not mention or is related to illegal immigrants these days. Only a few days ago were the RM950, 000.00 Hollywood-style robberies in Tawau.

The public has no inkling of the progress of the deportation programmed. And what we frequently hear is some of those deported were found returning to Kota Kinabalu within days or can be as early the boat that shipped them to the island had returned to Kota Kinabalu.

The attitude of the locals is equally upsetting. They allow foreigners to build houses on their land for a few ringgits.

The authorities or related agencies should come forward to explain to these people the repercussions of their doing. Even when the MPKK pulled the houses down the owners are actually liable to pay for expenses of pulling down the houses. But do they know that?

When I read that Pulau Gaya is slated to become the illegal immigrant's settlement, I consider it to be crazy and one of clear shortsightedness.

Pulau Gaya is known to be a transit safe heaven like for smugglers of cigarette and other items from Labuan before it finally reaches Kota Kinabalu. It is a common complaint from people living in this area that even government servants are involved indirectly in such activities.

When foreigners are given work pass to work in this country like in constructions industry, such work pass is only valid for specific time as per restriction in the Employment (Restriction) Act 1968 and Regulations 1969. Employer(s) must provide accommodation.

Employers must provide housing and other amenities to their employees. Such accommodation must meet the basic amenities like toilet, place for rubbish disposal, water and preventive measures of fire hazard and the like.

As observed and frequently highlighted in the media there are still quite a large number of employers who do not provide such facilities to their workers. The employers are violating the law, and liable to fine or imprisonment for failure of providing such accommodation.

Another example that I came across many times to date, where civil servants or Taukays who employ *amah*(s)—can be more than one amah does not even have passports or work pass. How do we expect the least educated citizens or the foreigners to respect the law when the privileged members of the society are purposely flouting the law? Some local or government officers keep these female illegal immigrants as mistresses or wives.

There have been arguments, some say if these people are not employed the social problem could be worst, and our constructions industry would be in jeopardy. I think we do have a fair idea about it but there is a need to weigh the cost and benefit for the interest of the country and the people in long term.

One can take notice during the morning rush hour several vans, buses or pickups either loading or unloading people across the town. These employers are acting like pirates. Sometimes among themselves they are pinching each other's workers. The workers do switch for various reasons. And this is against the Employment Act 1968. The employers are liable to be fined and the worker likewise is subject to deportation.

Majorities of Sabahans say social problems in the state now are at the critical stage. Apart from illegal housing incidents like robbery, thieving, forging ICs, drug taking, illegal hawking, rubbish dumping, etc are near to unmanageable stage.

27. THE SIPITANG 'TRAGEDY'-ROAD TO

27th December 1998

IT IS difficult to believe road to Sipitang is that bad. But yes, it is true. To some people who know nothing about it and never experience travelling to this part of the world will just say it is a gravel road, is it not?

Gravel is one thing, but the condition is another. For Sipitang people who commute in and out of the district, this is no laughing matter. The agony is beyond imagination especially, in the era of Malaysia acclaimed to be world class of sophistication, owning the world's tallest building and has the most modern airport, just to name a few. It is absurd. Malaysia also owns Sipitang; the world's worst inter state's highway.

Sabah gained its independent through Malaysia 35 years ago this year. It is very hard to understand why Sipitang people have to suffer this long. Most towns in Sabah have already achieved a reasonable improvement to their roads.

Even in remote areas most main roads have been uplifted beyond basic.

Every five year, Sabah holds its State general election. Every last five years, politician promised that road from Beaufort to Sipitang would be sealed.

Politicians never failed to promise, but they failed to deliver what they promise.

All too common excuses once elected are, 'this is not my jurisdiction, this is belong to YB that and YB this or this is Federal matter Not State's matter!' One will hear this finger pointing remarks from time to time by politicians.

Sipitang town is located at Brunei Bay, only about 145 km from Kota Kinabalu, and about 20km south of Beaufort town. The construction of inter state highway (Beaufort to Sipitang) cannot be too much difficult than any other roads in Sabah. Going towards Sipitang only two bigger hills two main bridges.

Now sealed roads from Kuching, to Sipitang and from Temburong, to Sipitang have been through. They have beautiful road. It is a common to see cars with Sarawak and Brunei plate numbers, park in front of Parkson Grand, Kota Kinabalu these days, where the owners are doing their shopping, especially on Sunday.

For the Brunei people spending money in Sabah would not be a bad choice because of the currency rate of exchange is in their favour.

The size of Sipitang district is about 1,055 square miles. It has about 28,000[47] inhabitants; about 60% are Kadayan, 30% Lundayeh and Murut, and 10% Brunei and Chinese and the rest. There are 10,946-registered voters[48].

The town is about 4 km to the border between Sabah and Sarawak at Sindumin, not only physically closed to Sarawak and Brunei; the people are originated from these places.

Labuan is another closely associated with Sipitang only about half an hour by boat. Majority of the Kadayan, Lundayeh and Brunai have relatives in Brunei, Sarawak and Labuan.

Sipitang people largely are farmers; vegetables' growers, padi planters nearly 75% and some are involved in fishing, those live in the seaside. But fishermen do not get much fish nowadays. I was informed that, the sea gets toxicated[49]. Many unspecified marine lives could have been killed; as a result of Sabah Forest Industry releasing its chemical waste to the sea, no study has ever been conducted so far and should be a good case study for UMS researchers.

Sabah Forest Industries, a paper and pulp industry created in 1984, the main jobs provider for about 3,000 folks but the actual number but the actual number of Sipitang people employed is negligible.

---

47.   Jabatan Perangkaan Malaysia, 1990
48.   Registered Voters in the last Sabah State General Election 1994
49.   I was informed by fishermen from Kg. Pelakat in 1997

For a record below is the list of very important people of Sipitang. First MP was the late Tuan Haji Abd Rashid Haji Jais, who held the MP seat for Ulu Padas (Sipitang and Tenom state constituencies), for 12 years until 1975.

The first Sipitang's State Assemblyman was Datuk Haji Mohd Yassin Haji Hashim who held it for nearly 13 years from 1963 to 1976. He was also a State Minister of Welfare in 1964, Minister for Co-ordination, and Minister of Finance under UNSO government and once Acting TYT.

The second Tuan Yang Terutama of Sabah (TYT) was Tun Pengiran Haji Ahmad Raffaee who was born in Sipitang. The First State Speaker State Assembly, post independent was Datuk Haji Kassim Haji Hashim, who held the post from 1967 until 1975. He had also been the *Yang Dipertua* MUIS, the younger brother of Datuk Haji Mohd Yassin.

Datuk Harris Mohd Salleh the former Chief Minister of Sabah was once an Assemblyman for Sipitang in 1967 and MP for Ulu Padas (Sipitang and Tenom) in 1978 and in 1982. He was the ADO for Sipitang in 1960.

The second Assemblyman was Tuan Haji Maidan Haji Jais who won the state general election in 1976 under USNO's ticket. Haji Ramli Dua 1982-1983 and Ibrahim Haji Ahmad 1984-1985, both were assemblymen under BERJAYA.

Datuk Haji Jawawi Haji Isa who was elected under USNO's ticket but crossed over to PBS in 1985. He held the assemblyman position until he died 1988. His wife Datin Jamilah Sulaiman, was elected as the state Assemblywoman for PBS, who won the sympathy of the people over the death of her husband in the by election. She held the Assist Minister post for nearly two terms.

Now the BN government, Datuk Sapawi Haji Ahmad is the Assemblyman for Sindumin (new name) who won in the state general election. He holds an Assistant Minister to the Chief Minister portfolio. He was also the *Yang Dipertua* of MUIS-Majlis Ugama Islam Sabah as of writing.

Datuk Dr Haji Yussuf Yakob stood for state general election twice but lost each time, until he switched for MP, now he is the MP for Sipitang constituency that covers Sipitang and Lumadan area.

The neighbour, Lumadan's Assemblywoman, Datuk Hajjah Dayang Mahani Tun Pengiran Ahmad Raffee once the State Minister of Communication and Works until1997, is also very close connected to Sipitang.

Hence, Sipitang does not lack in leadership and representatives, far better than many constituencies in Sabah.

In 1994 BN promised that, the road would be completely sealed in three years. Now their term is almost completed, but not the road. Whatever the reason, it is very unlikely that the road from Bukau to Mesapol will be sealed by the end of their term in March 1999.

The crucial part of the road that needs sealing is less than 20 km at the moment. I saw new notice board has just been erected recently somewhere near the Tropical Fruits farm, which says, "expected to be completed by the year 2001". Compare this road to the road going to Kota Belud, how long did they take to build?

That 20km road (some 10km is muddy, rocky and slippery) is worst in the rainy season. Imagine walking upstream in a rocky river or driving with an ordinary car. Driving with 4-wheel drive is the only option, while flying by helicopter is the VIPs' choice.

According to politicians' tenders for the construction and sealing of the road has been long awarded. The writer used to talk to the then Minister of Communication, according to her; the construction comes in 3 phases. The first was, the 7 km from Beaufort town to Bukau. The second was, from Bukau to Lingkongan and the third, from Lingkongan to Mesapol, Sipitang.

The works started off in 1995 include clearing, widening, shortening and cutting meanders of the current road. 1998 would complete a lot of talk about the sealing.

By 1997, the first phase the 7 kilometres was more or less done *forget* the quality. One of the two bridges was built as scheduled. The second phase of the road is on going but very incremental. The third phase is nothing moving at all.

The location of Sipitang town is very ideal as meeting point of the three states, plus it is close to Labuan. It is a gateway town.

Good road means; not only it is good for Sipitang people in particular, but for Sabah and Malaysia as a whole. Tourism and barter trades are among the most potential attraction; it will make Sipitang a boomtown, just needing a little bit of intuition.

There are one or two waterfalls, many beautiful unspoilt kampongs in the interior along the boarder between Sabah and Kalimantan one example is Long Pa Sia. A lot historical[50] places connecting Brunei and Sabah. Sipitang is the state representative for *gasing* team competition ever since.

Sipitang is well known for its *durian, rambutan* and *langsat* now coming up is sayur *Manis* getting plentiful, and cheap. Sipitang people supply Brunei and Labuan with these products.

---

50. Amde Sidik, "The Kadayan People" unpublished materials, 1998

Therefore, it is very difficult to understand why so little progress has made concerning the road. It is shameful for politician putting blame on one another. Whoever is given political power should take initiative regardless what portfolio one is holding. In certain situation consorted effort has to be required in order to make thing happen.

Given the scenario above, Sipitang has got reasonably educated representatives both in the State and Federal level. But education alone without wisdom does not make a man good and effective politician in this context.

It is fairly obvious from history, that this important road had never been the priority of political leaders in Sipitang.

*The Beaufort-Sipitang highway was eventually completed in 2001. What a sigh of relief to us. After nearly 36 years. When nearly all the major roads in Sabah were already sealed.

The Federal Minister of Communication Dato Seri Sammy Vellu visited several times to check the progress.

The writer has been very grateful to Director of RTM-Radio Television Malaysia Sabah Encik Jumaat Anson who indirectly assisted the writer to highlight the Sipitang Highway. Thanks to those who supported by writing to newspapers.

Socio-legal

28. Commissions of Inquiry

23rd January 2000

THE TERM, Commissions of Inquiry has been very widely used these days by politicians, by the media, and by the general public. Lawyers and law graduates have no problem in understanding it: the topic—Inquiry, is studied during their undergraduate stage either in the public law subject or in the administrative law subject.

My writing here is just to highlight the term, suffice to say, to provide general understanding what commissions of inquiry means, without involving technicality.

To inquire means to investigate or to find out more. The need of inquiry is because there is or are disputes over the resolution of something. A typical of Inquiry is to hear evidence and find facts, and the person/s conducting it finally make a recommendation to a minister and as how the minister should act again, depends on the policy of the government of the day.

Nearly similar but not exactly is tribunal—finds facts and decided the case by applying legal rules laid down by statute or regulations.

In many countries statutory inquiry is the standard device for giving a fair hearing to objectors before the final decision is made on some questions of government policy affecting citizen's rights or interests.

In England, anything that is very public in nature can amount to the setting up of Commissions of Inquiry. Such inquiry connotes upon the request by the Queen, the head of the state.

In Malaysia, the Commissions of Inquiry is made by the request of the Agong but in reality is a request by the concerned public-it reflects to be of the mood of the general public. Since the King represents the people, it is only rightly that the King wants to make sure that his subjects are fairly and justly judged—that is the moral idea.

For any Commissions of Inquiry to be set up, it must be of significant importance to general public. Inquiries are part of the procedure for ensuring that administrative power is fairly and reasonably exercised so that they have the same purpose as the legal principles of natural justice.

H.W.R.Wade, in the Administrative Law says, an enquiry means of dispensing justice without legal trimmings. It is part of the development of administration of justice for settling disputes without having to go to formal court of law.

It is rather difficult to pin point exactly how it starts and who tells the King, except, based on the 'democratic' way. The normal flow of decision, in Malaysia, it looks none other than the Prime Minister indirectly or otherwise, or at least upon his agreement. The Commissions of Inquiry Act, 1950 (Revised-1973) in fulfilment of Section 2(1), which states, govern the setting up of commissions of Inquiry:

The Yang Di Pertuan Agong may, where it appears to him to be expedient so to do, issue a Commission appointing one or more commissioners and authorizing the Commissioners to enquire into—

    a.   *the conduct of any federal officer;*

    b.   *the conduct or management of any department of the public service of the Federation;*

    c.   *conduct or management of any public institution which is not solely maintained by the state funds; or*

    d.   *any other many in which the inquiry would, in the opinion of the Yang di-Pertuan Agong, be or public welfare, not being—*

        1.   *a matter involving any question relating to the Muslim religion or the Malay custom; or*

        2.   *in relation to Sabah Sarawak; a matter specified in item 10 of the state list...*

One would see a wide range of subjects except for Section 2 (1)(d) (i)&(ii) above.

Under section 3(1) subject of the enquiry is specified, the subject of the enquiry and may in the discretion of the Yang di-Pertuan Agong, as the case may be, as per Section 3(1)(a)

There is no mentioned though how, what are the criteria and what are taken into account in the appointment of the rest of the members of the commissions, and much of the descriptions of the act is on how the commission conducts it business, except section 3(1)(a)

If there is more than one Commissioner, direct—

1. *the number of Commissioners which shall constitute a quorum*

2. *Which Commissioner shall be the Chairman; and*

My argument is, for any Public Inquiry to hold waters the public must have trust and confidence on the people who are appointed. This is nothing more important other than sticking to the established procedures though; the established procedures are not as straightforward as written law—refer to English model.

The Basic rules are to ensure one get a fair hearing. Thus any inquires that have powers to make decisions affecting an individual's welfare must abide by certain basic rules of fair play known as Natural Justice.

To be biased. If one has got an interest to the outcome of the decision he or she should not participate in the making of the decision.

For example, an officer cannot be junior in ranking to sit in the committee, which presides over a higher-ranking officer. Or say, a junior judge sits in the inquiry that presides over the dismissal of a senior judge.

Evidence must not be given behind your back and one must be allowed to put his or her own side of the case in his or her own way and his or her own time.

Failing short, any of those would make it difficult for people to see that the team of inquirers has arrived at the credible and unbiased findings.

The unbiased findings could only be obtained if the inquirers are of independence, not only in mind but also in real application, for example, the composition of the commission's members.

It is the cardinal rules that; justice should not only be done, but should manifestly and undoubtedly be seen to be done.

Many good examples that Public Inquiry served it purpose well, like finding out why disasters had happened, the collapsed of high rise building, railways crushed, the sinking of ship, plane exploded in mid air and so on.

But there were also quite a number of cases where public inquiry was conducted in an arbitrary manner by disregarding the rules. Lawyers and judges are supposed to be guidance of law but in many occasions, lawyers and judges break the rules, for reasons only known to them.

The most common problems that lead to the unsatisfactory outcome of many inquiries were due to failure of not following the established procedures.

In our context, I dare to say that politics somehow plays a big role in determining the outcome. We have seen this happened. It is because the authority wants to win too.

The right to a fair hearing-*audi alteram partem* hear the other side. This is a far reaching of the principles of natural justice; it embraces questions on fair procedure, or due process.

This is a very universal concept even in a developed system court of law in the world could extend without strictly follow the court established model.

I would think if for the better of mankind in seeking justice let it be.

In Malaysia, the most recent case was the inquiry as why the former Deputy Prime Minister Dato Seri Annuar Ibrahim got the black eye while in police custody. The findings did bring some answers.

I consider such inquiry could ease the public suspicion against the authority, but all too often, the authority would not like to commission any inquiry if they think the outcome is not in their favour.

This should not happen anymore being responsible government. And by continue denying citizen's right, could be seen rather as a sign of failure of the government in their practice of upholding the rule of law.

The rule of natural justice simply means, in natural sense of what is right and wrong.

In the administrative law of natural justice this concept has two fundamental rules of fair procedures:

- Man may not be a judged in his own cause
- Man's defence must always be fairly heard

Nemo judex in re sua—No man a judge in his own cause, a judge is disqualified for determining any case in which he may be, or may fairly be suspected to be biased.

In our case, justice system is compatible with any other developed nations in as far as theory is concerned or at least it claimed to be one. But the application of rule of law is still much to be desired.

The concept of separation of power appears to be not separated at all in practice.

In the inquiry of former Lord President Tun Salleh Abbas was a good example, why a person who got the interest to be the next Lord President set in the panel that made decision and why a junior ranking judge/s set to preside over the fate of Lord President. As mentioned earlier there is no law to tell who and how to appoint the members of the commissions but it is in every lawyers or judges knowledge such an act ought to be seen bias by one way or the other.

The government can have thousand committees when at the end one person decides.

For any Inquiry to be of any benefit, it must be done as what it should be done. Many more we hear these days that the authority wants to commission the inquiry for this and that. But the purpose is not for scoring political mileage, because it involves people welfare, people at large want to know what exactly happened. Who caused it to happen?

Recently, there was an outcry for a commission of inquiry to be conducted in Sabah with regard to the illegal immigrants.

The authority should not take this lightly by saying no, just because the opposition political party highlighted it.

The outcome of such inquiry could be useful in the formulation of strategies; to counter the persisting problem—this is also an issue of transparency.

29. UNCLAIMED MALAYSIANS IDENTITY CARDS

27 June 1999

THERE are 34,442 unclaimed ICs in Sabah alone, as of April 1999 (The Daily Express, June 14th, 1999), according to the Director General of the National Registration Department—NRD Datuk Azizan Ayub.

These ICs are going to be destroyed by October, if remain uncollected for 18 months from the date of issuance.

Section 6, of the National Registration Act 1959, refers to the *Regulation 26(1) of National Registration Regulations 1990, says,...the DG may dispose of any identity card issued to any person if it has not been collected by the person to whom it was issued, after due notice....*

In the sub-regulation (2) Any identity card shall be retained for a period of not less than 18 months from the date it was issued or such longer period as the DG may direct and at such registration office as he may specify, unless sooner collected by the person to whom it was issued.

The sub-regulation (3)...The DG shall a cause a notice to be given, in such manner and form as the DG deems fit and proper, to the person to whom the identity cards was issued to collect the same on or before the date as may be specified in the notice.

No specific provision mentioned in the regulations as to how the DG shall a cause a notice, or the extend of activities involved to notify the owner before the 18 months period expires. The NRD relies on the Regulation 24(1) on no presumption as to the correctness of information provided by the applicant at the time he or she applied, where the burden of proving as to correctness of the contents includes address and the like, shall be on the applicant.

But relying on Regulation 24(1) alone has not proven to be effective in many ways, and the tests of its reliability has manifested in so many forms and so many occasions, one knows, it is subjective, because it is only human?

The Act gives very wide discretion to the Director General. The General Public[1] therefore, will not know exactly how much efforts has been made by the NRD officers before the ICs are finally destroyed. The General Public has no access to inspect the register by law, except, authorized by DG, under regulation 12(2) or empowered by Chapter XIII of the Criminal Procedure Code for the police.

The reason of wanting to destroy according to the Director General is, because of thefts, some 1000 KPTS have been stolen from the NRD offices.

Are all the unclaimed ICs to be recalled at one centre, once an 18th months period is over? Based on Regulation 26(2) it does not need, it is up to the discretion of the individual office, that is, the DG.

I am not questioning the wisdom of the officials here, but I am worried about the method of destroying, the standard procedures might not be adhered to. In other words, how are these ICs being destroyed?

Every one knows that Malaysians ICs are like hot cakes, and always in high demand. Forgeries[2] are rampant. Both genuine and fake ICs were sold to illegal immigrants. There were cases in the past where NRD staffs were found abusing their position in administering[3] the ICs. Certain leaders and politicians[4] were involved in selling and distributing genuine and non-genuine ICs to foreigners and placed under ISA.

This is no longer a secret. In the eyes of the public, the authorities concerned have not been seen 'very serious' in wanting to solve these problems, based on the

---

1. General ordinary people, not those who hold power like, executives in the government or politicians.
2. Cases on forgeries have been frequently reported in the local media.
3. Example of a civil servant involved; found to have kept acknowledgement receipts of identity card and NRD stamp in his house.
4. It is already in public knowledge that some local politicians were involved and were detained under ISA

incidents that, illegal immigrants were given genuine ICs and the ever increase of fake ICs around. The ICs issue is too important to be ignored.

The government officers must not act arbitrarily like, going for a quick solution. Some unscrupulous politicians[5] and local leaders had been involved for the sake of quick money, status and power.

The NRD is proposing to impose penalty to applicants, who are not collecting their ICs in time, because it costs money to make those ICs. I wonder if such strategy will work, because even when no fine is imposed they still do not come to collect.

The Sabah NRD's Director, Datuk Ibrahim Haji Jusuh said, that 52,320 new high-security[6] ICs remained unclaimed as of February this year since 1991. The Department has issued repeated reminders including press statement. I would suggest this is a good case for University students or the relevant bodies, to undertake studies to find out what are the main cause(s) for not collecting.

Assumptions

Something must have gone wrong somewhere, between the owners and the makers of the ICs. My assumptions are as follows:

- The applicants, do not know that their ICs have arrived[7]

- The applicants have not been informed that their ICs are ready for collection or the information about their ICs has not reached the applicants.

- The applicants must be living very deep in the interior or elsewhere where no means of communication could reach them.

- The applicants are not interested in getting their ICs, and if that is the case, most likely they are not bona fide applicants so they are not Malaysian (Sabahan)

- The applicants either have died or migrated elsewhere:

- Method(s) of informing or notifying the applicants (owners) are not good enough on the part of NRD.

---

5. *ibid*

6. Daily Express, reported in June, 1999

7. Note: A simple study has been conducted by asking question randomly.
    Questions: how easy was it to collect the IC? And was it in time? 17 of 20 said, not that simple as claimed that reported in the media. It takes months if not years before the ICs are ready. Very often requires more than one visit.

- The Regulation 4 is a not good enough for obtaining the authenticity of information from the applicants.

- Method(s) of ascertaining information from the application is not good enough.

That the IC is such precious document, a Malaysian not having one is like a 'criminal' on the run. Therefore, I do not see any good reason for any bona fide Malaysian for not collecting his or her IC. Without IC, one is losing many of privileges and also cannot exercise many of his or her legal rights, as a citizen.

Malaysians in Sabah, in particular, have every reason to be concerned about the staggering numbers of uncollected ICs, when the number of illegal immigrants is swelling to more than half a million, with a ratio of 1:2 against the local. In my view, tracing the owners is still the best solution. The NRD has to device a system locating and finding these people.

Skepticism

There are many factors why the public is sceptical about the way the authorities handle this issue. The classical example is the availability of ICs either genuine or forged ICs every time at the eve of State general election[8].

The common source is the electoral roll[9] where many names appeared sharing the same number of ICs or the same name appears holding more than one IC.

A remark[10] by the NRD official a few days before the State General Election 1999, that the Department has not got sufficient manpower to check, did not bring much comfort either to majority of the people in Sabah.

In such incident, the NRD cannot be considered to have made a bona fide mistake, when such mistake occurred too frequent.

The making of forged ICs is not within the NRD controlled, but the question is, why is it so easy to forge? Besides the IC, is the birth certificate, stamped with late registration? An example is my former maid who newly arrived[11] from Indonesia got a late registration of birth certificate; her place of birth is Suang Prai just behind the famous spiral building—Sabah Foundation.

When asked about the place, she could not even tell where. How did she get that piece of certificate?

---

8.   Common knowledge; see also Mutalib Mohd Daud, *IC Palsu, 1999*
9.   Example in the last Sabah State electoral roll of 1999, see also Mutalib Mohd Daud, *IC Palsu, 1999*
10.   Daily Express report 1999
11.   This is a case of the writer's former *amah* who was just arrived from Sulawasi.

An ordinary person on the street would not be able to tell the different between the original and fake accept, the issuing Department.

Mutalib Mohd Daud in his book *'IC Palsu-Merampas Hak Anak Sabah' 1999*, has provided substantial reference materials pertaining to this issue except that, the contents of the book is very massy and has not been properly presented.

Mutalib claimed that politicians[12] are the biggest culprits in making ICs available to the illegal immigrants. They do it in order to enable them (the illegal immigrants) to vote in the State General Election, very commonly called phantom voters[13].

If this is true I am not surprised as to why the illegal immigrants wanted revenge, and even dare to challenge (to kill) the MPKK officials who demolished their colony at kampong Manggorok[14] recently.

Or worst still, they even resorted to use the Istana[15] as their defence.

Coming back to the issue of unclaimed ICs, could it be that, some of these people have been deported? As reported in the media recently, they were 34,342 have been deported.

I am not saying all but at least some? If this theory is right, the NRD officers have not done their job properly in identifying the real Sabahan.

The irony is many Sabahan or Sarawakian in remote places is still wandering around in the 'jungle', stateless, without ICs.

The Orang Ulu such as in Belaga, Ulu Baram and Lawas, about 7000[16] of them are yet to possess valid documents, birth certificate and identity cards.

For them living in the jungle does not require IC.

I traveled quite extensively to remote areas of Sabah in1997 the interior of Kota Marudu and Pensiangan, Tenom and Sipitang and came across Sabahan who still do not have ICs.

When asked they said when the mother delivered the baby at home they did not report it for registration. The parents only realise that the kid needs to have an IC by the time he or she is about to sit for SRP examination.

In some cases, the parent has died the kid has been looked after by the relatives. A Lundayeh girl was born in Sabah but the parent preferred to stay in Kalimatan (Indonesia).

---

12.   Mutalib Mohd Daud, *IC Palsu*, 1999
13.   *ibid*
14.   Daily Express, June 21st, 1999
15.   Daily Express, June 22nd, 1999
16.   Borneo Mail, June 1999

This pure lack of understanding about the importance of having an IC on the part of the local people needs to be corrected. The relevant the authorities must take a proactive role to reach these people.

People of Sabah who live in the interior are less likely to be foreigners compare to those found living at the coastal part of Kota Kinabalu or coastal of the East Coast of Sabah.

A local grandmother was born in Sarawak but had been in Sabah for the last 60 years. She applied for an IC like anyone else for 'Warganegara' but received red IC, catogerised[17] as 'Penduduk Tetap', which by right she should get the former. She never had the blue ICs until she died.

Some illegal immigrants did not even apply[18] yet they get blue ICs. For a kampong folk, the task of rectifying a mistake like the above can be a nightmare[19], equipped with very little knowledge about civil servants' rituals.

He or she has to go up and down to look for NRD office and be subject to procedures.

The NRD's roles should be extended to providing like, teaching public, instilling awareness of the importance of having ICs, other government agencies, local leaders, politician, community leaders should come together.

There should be on-going exercise carried out by mobile registering team. Datuk Leo Moggie Energy, Communication and Multimedia Minister[20] commented that NRD should be flexible with the late registration application from the rural-based Sarawak native communities.

Special training or incentives may be given to the officers of NRD because it is only too easy for these people to be influenced by inducement.

This corrupt practice[21] has become so rampant, a number of local politicians had been detained for years under ISA but does this really deter them?

The law should be made stiffer for people committed this offence. There should be a provision in the law to make sure that their property earned by this means be confiscated by the authority.

I suggest that the authority should consider the followings:

---

17.   Regulation 5, National Registration Regulations 1990, National Registration Act 1959
18.   Mutalib Mohd Daud IC *Palsu*, 1999
19.   This is a common saying see also Forum, Daily Express, June 20th, 1999
20.   Daily Express report, June 1999
21.   *Op.cit*

- There should be some expertise, special training given to officers in identifying the real bona fide Malaysian;

- Flexibility, based on the uniqueness of locality;

- There should be frequent visit to places in the interior;

- The NRD should take proactive role in assisting the less fortunate;

  and

- Other bodies or agencies should play a role for example, ketua kampong, local politicians and teachers a like.

Hence, while some locals suffer of having no ICs and other having to wait for many years, the illegal immigrants are seizing the opportunity as fast as they can. Of course, this could not be done so without the assistant of unscrupulous individuals.

The districts NRD have to do some extra work, because the people should not be deprived of their rights to have ICs just because they are naive or ignorant.

Nature of the naiveté of people of Sabah and Sarawak has to be understood.

Destroying these unclaimed ICs, if it is done hastily, not only will complicate the matters. We might one day find ourselves overdoing it and only to be blamed by our next generation.

30. Two sides of rotation issue of Chief Minister of Sabah

18 April 1999

MAJORITY of people of Sabah reluctant to agree to continue the rotation of the Chief Minister (CM) while substantial number agree and the rest cannot be bothered.

There are two ways of looking at this rotation issue—one is to do with logic, the other is to do with State constitutional issues.

The Prime Minister sees it fair to have Sabah CM rotated among the three major communities, namely, the Muslim, Kadazandusun and the Chinese, for the duration of two years each.

Except that, one term of governance is only 5 years. Thus, the third CM will most likely to get less than 2 years, Tan Sri Dompok was an example.

Rotation issue started as an election promise of 1994, in the state general election. PM promised to have Sabah Chief Minister be rotated if BN won the general election.

BN did not win in the 1994 general election, but they formed the government because of the PBS assemblymen crossed over to BN components parties.

Do we consider the rotation of the CM is fair to every body, or only to specific groups?

Rotation is unnecessary as it complicates the administration of the state.

In the context of integration this is not healthy. In fact, it creates a bigger division among people.

Perpaduan briefly means all communities big or small are in one family. Their integration is due the understanding of each other regardless of their origins.

When applying the rotation concept, it looks the political master is focusing only to specific groups. It is unfair, and divisive.

An acceptable leader does not have to be identified from whose community he is. Many examples in the world where people live on communal based, very often led to a never ending communal warfare, Bosnia, Kosovo, some in African states, and or our nearest neighbour, Indonesia is among the examples.

Our integration in Sabah has a sound foundation; it has been here as long as we could remember and without anyone telling us what to do. The introduction of rotation is therefore clock backward.

I agree we have had 'unstable' leadership over the years but this is rather the problem of political leaders not about the disintegration of masses.

This second part of my argument is to touch briefly on the constitutional issues.

Our country has written constitutions like many other modern countries, which is founded on the rule of law[22].

The primarily means everything must be done according to law.

For example when applying the power of government, that government must act only within the authorised by the constitution (by the law)

There is a fine line between the principle of legality and the executives unrestricted discretionary power, even though the requirement that everything done must be within the law. *Quod principi placuit legis habet vigorem*—the sovereign's will has the force of law.

So, there can be a rule by arbitrary power rather the rule according to ascertainable law. Many classic examples in the old England, the Home Secretary had

---

22.   Definition by Dicey, the *Law of Constitution*

unlimited power to revoke any television licence and local planning authority made planning permission if it thinks fit.

But the court of justice will not allow the these powers to be used in ways which Parliament is not thought to have intended, by applying the standard of reasonableness in other words, within the bounds of legal reasonableness. Some say, the decision is unlawful if it is one to which no reasonable authority could have come.

Our constitution has no provision to accommodate the practice of rotation of Chief Minister.

Constitution is protected by fundamental law for example against amendment not at least voted for by 2/3 majority in our case, power of executive here subject to due process of law.

All matters to do with the appointment of CM is vested in Article 6(3) which says,

"TYT shall appoint as CM, a member of Legislative Assembly who in his judgement is likely to command the confidence of a majority of the members of the Assembly"

The Article 6(2) appointment of the rest of the members of the Assembly.

First, The Tuan Yang Terutama (TYT) appoints CM. TYT can dismiss CM? Under Article 7, *if the CM ceases to command the confidence of a majority of the members of the Legislative Assembly, then, unless at his request the TYT dissolves the Assembly, the CM shall tender the resignation of the members of the Cabinet.* Which also means CM holds office under the pleasure of TYT, thus applies other the rest of members of the cabinet.

That means, any appointment which is made outside the provision of the constitution is not legal, what would be the status of his administration, would it void?

If the TYT says that the CM appointment is only for two years and the appointment has to come to end at the end of two years. There is no provision to this point, and if TYT made that such appointment, this is beyond what the constitution can allow him to do.

Our Federal constitution gives power to TYT to agree for any law under which has been approved by the Dewan but not otherwise.

Ronny Cham, Daily Express, March 28, 1999 in "Take Mustapha case as cue" touched on the supremacy of state constitution, where he said, rotation system is not contained in the state constitution but was done as a matter of expediency.

I will say, by forgoing the legal procedure and replaces it with the arbitrary act, is a slap to our democracy.

31. PARDON OR NO PARDON

29 February 2004

There have been some contentions in the media about Datuk Yong Teck's intention to reapply for Royal pardon recently.

Datuk Mohd Fauzi Patel in his column two weeks ago (what is really behind the pardon move) commented that there's nothing more Datuk Yong Teck Lee could do. It is a cul-*de sac*, no matter how he corners.

My view is that Datuk YTL should be quiet and wait until the time-barred expires.

Patel spelt out the reasons why YTL should not proceed with his petition to get Royal pardon. If indeed he proceeds and eventually gets it, in Patel's opinion it is bad for BN, bad for justice system and bad for the country.

Another reasons, if YTL is given Royal Pardon such decision is considered unfair to others, creates a precedent that executive interfere with judicial process. And it will validate the misguided belief that the PM gets a Royal Pardon. That would damage the election court system.

But that is Patel's opinion.

It would be interesting to see more views, after all this is a matter of public interest. It is only fair that public is well informed especially those voted in Likas constituency. And the voters should be given choice to think rather than coerced to think. Is this not an issue of transparency?

Just to recapture, Datuk Yong Teck Lee was found guilty by the Election Court in Kota Kinabalu in 2001 for an offence called *corrupt practice* that the billboard erected by him did not bear the source of name and address of the origin.

As penalty, he had to relinquish the seat. He is barred from standing in any state election for YB until the year 2006; this is in accordance with the provision in our Federal Constitution.

It means, he is not allowed to participate in this upcoming state general election unless of course he is given a Royal pardon.

Many would ask—is this pardonable case for the Pardon Board? Meaning, his offence is one of the kind, which Pardon Board could consider. Why? Because there's no mention in our Federal constitution about election offences, only for criminal cases and those tried by court-martial.

YTL applied to the Pardon Board in 2002, and rejected.

Our Federal Constitution also does not mention that those whose application was rejected could not re-apply. Also no time limit or how many time one could apply. This is where I think, keep on trying is still the best strategy for him.

The Pardon Board is created in this manner; our supreme law—Federal Constitution provides the establishment of Royal Pardon Board under Section 42, Power of Pardon, which says, *The Yang di Pertuan Agong and the TYT have power to grant pardons, reprieves and respites in respect of all offences which have tried my court-martial [and all offences committed in the Federal][Territories of Kuala Lumpur and labaun]; and the Ruler or TYT of a state has power to grant pardons, reprieves and respite in respect of all other offences committed in his state.*

There had been some kind of confusion in the early stage of YTL's application. General public in the state was given the impression that there is no provision in the Federal Constitution for Royal pardon for election offences.

The then Chief Minister of Sabah Datuk Chong Kah Kiat[23] even made announcement several times saying that there was no provision in the Constitution for Royal Pardon. He had said it was only applicable in the case of election agent committing an offence or and situation where offence was committed before Malaysia day.

In my opinion, the provision in that Section 42 of the Federal Constitution includes any other offences. There is no more heinous offence than criminal offences for example, murder or rapist, if those offences are received by Pardon Board I see no reason the lesser offence is not entertained for consideration.

The rest of the article states how and who are the Board members.

With regard to the Sabah, the TYT presides the Board proceeding. The Board consists of Federal AG, CM and three other members appointed by TYT. One can therefore see who influences who.

The term of appointment of the Board Members is three years though they are eligible for reappointment.

The current composition of the Sabah Royal Pardon Board is obviously different then when YTL last applied. This is because we have new TYT, new CM and one member had passed away that must be replaced by new person.

Thus, the make up of the Board substantively different. And I am of the opinion again that no two people have exactly the same mind, thought they may agree but not necessarily because of the same reason.

---

23. News Sabah Times (14.09.2002), Borneo Post (14.09.2002) and New Straits Times (14.09.2004)

The Board is not discussing about legal matters but rather on the ground of mercy on humane. The discussion obviously is not as rigid as discussing legal matters.

The Pardon Board is only an advisory body and makes no decision whatever as such but only tenders advise to Yang di Pertuan Agong or the Ruler of a State or TYT for the purpose of the exercise of the power of clemency[24].

In the course of my researching for materials for this article I found a few press statements made by politicians and lawyers alike, were a bit inconsistent and odd for those familiar with interpretations of law.

My impression is, the State pardon Board in 2002 never had it on agenda because it "thought" it had no jurisdiction [against the unambiguous provision in the Federal Constitution] even to the extent that one pardon board member publicly pre empted the result of the petition[25].

The very function and duty of the Royal Pardon Board is to hear application for clemency from those committed offences particularly criminal offences. But it is only logical that among the basis of consideration is taking stock on the gravity of offence.

For the interest of general public, that election offence is lesser than those I have already mentioned. This is where I think there is no harm for YTL or for anybody else to apply or reapply petition for Royal pardon.

Whether the move to reapply petition in the case of YTL is politically motivated or otherwise is not for me to say but my view is purely from looking at the constitution, whose function is to guarantee and safeguard the interest of the people of the country.

The establishment of Royal Pardon Board is a clear example of the intention of our constitution to give the last chance even for a criminal.

As commonly quoted[26] 'Mercy is not the subject of legal rights. It begins where legal rights end'

'...the power of mercy is a high prerogative power exercisable by the Yang di Pertuan Agong or the Ruler of a state or the Yang di Pertuan Negeri...who acts with the greatest conscience and care and without fear influence from any quarter'

---

24. Superintendent of Pudu Prison & Ors v Sim Kie Chon [1986]
     1 MLJ 494 (SC)
25. New Sabah Times, (By Afeza Khan) 14.09.2002
26. Chiow Thiam Guan v Superintendent of Pudu Prison and the Government of Malaysia [1983] 2 MLJ 116

Biography

Amde Sidik is a guest columnist with Daily Express and correspondent for Malaysiakini.com. He holds BA, MSc, LLB degrees from England and his legal practice from Australia. Former Senior Manager, Senior Legal Officer of Sabah Foundation and President of Sabah's Kedayan Association. He lectures law at local University in Sabah.

Glossary of Translations

Merdeka	independent
Gawat	emergency
Kaamatan	cultural/religious festival
Pisang goring	fried banana
Tasak lasak	durable
Batang buruk	local cake
Kayu balak	timber logs
Wargakota	city dwellers
Amah	housemaid
Gerai	open-air canteen
Lanun	pirate
Dewan Rakyat	assembly hall
Pesta	celebration
Persatuan	association
Kampong	village
Kedai kopi	coffee shop
Tambadau	rhinoceros
Payau	reindeer
Tea tarik	tea making—Malaysia style.
Boleh	can be done
Wakil	representative
Rakyat	people/cltlzenz
Songkok	cap

Ceramah	*talk*
Berpadu	*integration*
Angkat kaki	*blowing oneself/others*
Sokong	*support*
Cuba-cuba	*tries*
Tamu	*trade gathering for locals*
Angan-angan	*imagination*
Parang	*machete*
Yang Di Pertua	*head of...*
Bersopan	*polite*

0-595-32657-9